OPEN LOOK®

GRAPHICAL USER INTERFACE

USER'S GUIDE

UNIX System Laboratories, Inc.

Published by Prentice Hall, Inc.
A Simon & Schuster Company
Englewood Cliffs, New Jersey 07632

IMPORTANT NOTE TO USERS

TRADEMARKS

ISBN 0-13-636267-2

UNIX
PRESS
A Prentice Hall Title

Contents

Figures and Tables

Table of Contents _____

1 Introduction

Introducing the OPEN LOOK Interface

The OPEN LOOK® Graphical User Interface is a software application that creates a user-friendly, graphical environment for the UNIX® Operating System. The OPEN LOOK Interface replaces many of the traditional UNIX System commands with three-dimensional graphics that include windows, menus, icons, and other symbols. Easy operations performed with a hand-held pointing device called a mouse allow you to manipulate all these features. You can also access these features from the keyboard, if you prefer not to use a mouse.

The OPEN LOOK Interface encompasses a wide range of features and capabilities. Once you learn to use the system and become familiar with even some of the features, you will see that operations such as menu selection are as simple as pointing at your choice and pressing a button on the mouse or keyboard.

OPEN LOOK Interface Features

The OPEN LOOK Interface includes the following applications.

- The Window Manager application (olwm)
- The Workspace Manager application (olwsm)
- The File Manager application (olfm)
- The Terminal Emulator application (xterm)
- The Print Screen application (olprintscreen)
- The Administration Manager (olam)
- The Pixmap Editor (olpixmap)

The Window Manager application and the Workspace Manager application are OPEN LOOK Interface programs that allow you to create and manipulate windows on your screen. The Window Manager provides the capability to create multiple windows, in which you can run any number of OPEN LOOK Interface applications, or other applications such as word processing programs, spreadsheet programs, or database managers. Any application you run on your computer can be run in an OPEN LOOK window. The Window Manager creates windows on your screen, with elements such as headers, window menus, and other features. You can open a window, move a window, change its size, run it in the background by converting it into an icon, restore the icon back to a full window, and then, of course, exit the window.

The Workspace Manager application provides the background screen area for displaying objects such as icons and the windows themselves. The workspace menu gives you access to the utilities and programs of the OPEN LOOK Interface, and also to the workspace property windows, with which you customize your environment.

The File Manager provides an easy-to-use interface to the UNIX Operating System. You can view your files, edit and execute UNIX System files, and traverse the file system without ever typing a command at the UNIX prompt. You just point to a menu selection and press a mouse button, or use the File Manager's "drag and drop" method, which lets you manipulate files, directories, and executables without a menu. If you prefer, you can also manipulate files with the "drag and drop" method using your keyboard, rather than a mouse. Additionally, you can move around the system, execute functions, and call up menus via the keyboard.

The Terminal Emulator application emulates the AT&T 6386 WGS (Work Group System) color console. You can run any application or program from a Terminal Emulator window. You can also perform any UNIX system command from the Terminal Emulator window, because it gives you access to the UNIX System prompt.

The Print Screen application incorporates the features of several XWIN Graphical Windowing System commands into the OPEN LOOK environment. This gives you an easy graphical method to display and print windows and portions of your OPEN LOOK screen.

The olpixmap application is a supported application intended for use mainly by software developers, but it is available to any user to create custom backgrounds. (Please note only dithered backgrounds are OPEN LOOK GUI specification compliant). See olpixmap(1) in Appendix A, "Supported Applications," if you want to use this application.

OPEN LOOK Interface Networking Capabilities

The OPEN LOOK Graphical User Interface Release 4 can be used by many individuals linked together in a networking environment. The OPEN LOOK Interface has networking capabilities so local and remote clients and servers can communicate over an Ethernet™ or StarLAN network.

The OPEN LOOK Interface is perfectly suited to the requirements of a distributed multi-user environment. It helps you share network resources by allowing access to hardware devices on other nodes — concurrently, through separate windows on your computer screen. It is device-independent and operating system-independent. With the OPEN LOOK Interface installed, an application is portable and can run within one operating system while displaying on another.

Administering these network connections is the function of the OPEN LOOK Administration Manager application. Like the other OPEN LOOK applications, the Administration Manager uses windows and menus to enable you to administer network connections to both the StarLAN Network and Ethernet.

Intended Audience

This manual contains information intended for both the novice user and the experienced user. The novice user is one with limited experience with both windowing systems and the UNIX System. The novice user will find useful information in Chapters 2 through 7 and the glossary. Chapter 9, "The Print Screen Application" and Chapter 10, "Troubleshooting," contain information valuable for all users.

The experienced user should already be familiar with the UNIX System. The experienced user may have system administrator privileges and may also install and configure the OPEN LOOK Interface. Information on administration and network connections are found in Chapter 8. The manual pages on supported applications in Appendix A contain more detailed information on the programs that comprise the OPEN LOOK Interface.

Document Overview

The *User's Guide* is organized into the following chapters:

- Chapter 1, Introduction. The introduction contains:

    □ Information about the OPEN LOOK interface and this guide.

    □ Document overview and conventions

- Chapter 2, Getting Started. This chapter describes how to use the OPEN LOOK Interface, including:

    □ Using the mouse

    □ Using keyboard equivalent functions

    □ A "getting started" tutorial with activities such as logging in and out, creating windows, and running applications

- Chapter 3, The OPEN LOOK Interface: Features. This chapter provides descriptions of the features that comprise the OPEN LOOK Interface. Sections of this chapter include information on:

    □ Windows and icons

    □ Controls and control areas

    □ Menus

- Chapter 4, The OPEN LOOK Interface: Procedures. This chapter supplies procedures for using the features of the OPEN LOOK Interface, including:

    □ Window operations

    □ Menu operations

    □ Scrollbars and scrolling

    □ Help messages

- Chapter 5, The Workspace Manager Application. This chapter describes the workspace property windows and how to use them.

- Chapter 6, The File Manager Application. This chapter describes the use of the File Manager application, which provides manipulation of UNIX System files and directories.

- Chapter 7, The Terminal Emulator Application. This chapter explains how to use the Terminal Emulator application, which provides a standard terminal type for applications not written specifically for the OPEN LOOK Interface environment. This application gives you the Terminal Emulator window, from which you can access the UNIX prompt and all other applications via UNIX commands.

- Chapter 8, The Administration Manager Application. This chapter describes how to use the Administration Manager application to administer remote host and display connections.

- Chapter 9, The Print Screen Application. This chapter explains how to use the Print Screen window to view and print screen dumps.

- Chapter 10, Troubleshooting. This chapter provides, in easy-to-read table format, answers to questions about problems you may encounter while using the OPEN LOOK Interface.

- Appendices. The appendices include the following:

  □ Appendix A contains manual pages for supported applications.

  □ Appendix B contains control sequences for xterm.

  □ Appendix C contains programming information for the File Manager application.

- Glossary. Provides definitions and explanations of words and phrases used in this guide.

Document Conventions

The *OPEN LOOK Graphical User Interface User's Guide* uses certain typographical conventions such as constant width and italics to identify different types of information. The following conventions apply:

- Commands that you must type on the computer exactly as shown appear in `constant width`.

- Variables to those commands appear in *italic*. For example, in the command

      xwd -out *filename*

  filename will be any name that you select as the file name to be entered.

- File names and programs appear in *italics*.

- Computer output such as prompts and messages appear in `computer style type`.

- Keyboard references are shown with the key graphic. (↵) and (ESC) are two examples. When you see a keyboard instruction such as "Press (CTRL) (w) " this means you must type (w) while holding down the (CTRL) key.

- The mouse buttons, SELECT, ADJUST, and MENU appear in all capital letters.

- Instructional procedures are divided into two parts. If you are using OPEN LOOK with a mouse, refer to the part of the procedure labelled "MOUSE;" if you are using a keyboard, refer to the part of the procedure labelled "KEYBD."

- Depending on whether you are using OPEN LOOK in 2D or 3D mode, the controls displayed on the screen may have a different visual appearance. If you are using 2D mode, the control becomes highlighted with the input focus color to indicate that it is the current control; if you are using 3D mode, the control has a "depressed" appearance. In this Guide, the term "selected" is used to refer to a control that has either a depressed or highlighted appearance.

2 Getting Started

Introduction

This chapter is designed to give you enough information to enable you to use the mouse and perform a few OPEN LOOK procedures before reading the rest of the manual.

Overview

The sections "Using the Mouse," "Using the Keyboard," and "Using the OPEN LOOK Interface" provide you with procedures which will enable you to use the mouse buttons or keyboard to access menus, close windows and open icons, and run an application. These sections should give you enough familiarity with the OPEN LOOK Interface so that you can understand the more detailed information in subsequent chapters.

Many of the terms used in this chapter will not be familiar to you at this point. The procedures in "Using the OPEN LOOK Interface" are meant to give you an introduction to the system, and contain no elaboration or definitions. Full detail is available in Chapters 3 and 4. You can also refer to the glossary in the back of this manual for definitions of unfamiliar words or phrases.

Organization of the Chapter

The contents of this chapter are arranged as follows:

- Using the Mouse.

  Explains how to use the mouse, the mouse pointer, and the SELECT, ADJUST, and MENU buttons.

- Using the Keyboard.

  Explains how to use the keyboard in place of the SELECT, ADJUST, and MENU buttons on the mouse.

- Keyboard Specifications.

  Defines keyboard equivalents for certain mouse button operations.

- Using the OPEN LOOK Interface.

  Supplies procedures for accessing menus, creating windows, running applications, and closing windows and opening icons.

Using the Mouse

A mouse is a hand-held pointing device used to manipulate windows and display and select items from the OPEN LOOK Interface menus. Moving the mouse across the work surface in front of your terminal controls the movement of the small symbol on the screen called the mouse pointer. You can perform functions by moving the pointer to a specific place on the screen and then pressing or clicking a mouse button to complete an action. Figure 2-1 shows a drawing of a typical three-button right-handed mouse. All functions that you perform with the mouse can also be accessed from the keyboard. See "Using the Keyboard" later in this chapter for more information.

Figure 2-1: Typical Three-Button Mouse

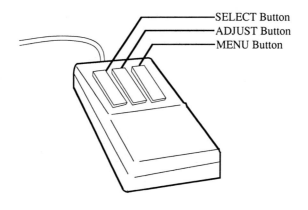

SELECT Button
ADJUST Button
MENU Button

The Mouse Buttons

The SELECT, ADJUST, and MENU buttons shown in Figure 2-1 each perform specific functions. The following table gives a brief synopsis of what each button does, as shown on a right-handed mouse. The mouse buttons throughout this manual are referred to as SELECT, ADJUST, and MENU, not left, center, and right.

Figure 2-2: Mouse Button Functions

Use This Mouse Button	Default Location	To Perform This Function
SELECT	On the left.	Select objects or manipulate objects and controls.
ADJUST	In the middle.	Add to or take away from a group of selected objects.
MENU	On the right.	Display and choose from menus.

NOTE The locations listed in the table above are the default locations. You can change the button locations if you wish. See the section "Mouse Modifiers Workspace Property Window" in Chapter 5 for information on setting the mouse buttons from the mouse settings workspace property window.

If you do not have a three-button mouse, see page 7 for information on using one or two button mice.

Mouse Usage Terminology

The mouse's purpose is to make it easy for you to manipulate windows and icons. Read the table in Figure 2-3 to familiarize yourself with the terms that define different mouse functions.

Figure 2-3: Mouse Usage Terminology

Term	Definition
Press	Press a mouse button down and hold it down without releasing it.
Release	Let go of the mouse button to initiate the action.
Click	Quickly press and release a mouse button before moving the pointer.
Double-Click	Quickly press and release a mouse button twice in succession without moving the pointer.
Multiple-Click	Quickly press and release a mouse button two or three times (double-click, or triple-click) in succession without moving the pointer.
Move	Move the pointer by sliding the mouse without pressing any buttons.
Drag	Slide the mouse while holding one or more buttons.

Shorthand conventions are used in this manual to refer to mouse button functions: for instance, "Click SELECT" means "Click the SELECT mouse button."

You may not understand all the terms used to describe the mouse button functions until you have read the subsequent information in this manual. Chapter 3 defines the window features. Chapter 4 describes how to use the mouse on windows and menus.

The SELECT Button

You perform the following with the SELECT button:

- Change the active input area from one window to another:

    Active input focus refers to the area of the screen that accepts input from the keyboard. To give a particular window active input focus, move the pointer to the header and click SELECT. When a window has active input focus, any characters you type automatically go to the application running in the window.

- Select controls:

  Clicking SELECT on a control such as a button will cause the control to perform its designated function.

- Increase or decrease the area of a window:

  To change the size of a window, press SELECT while dragging on a resize corner.

- Move a window or an icon:

  To move a window, press SELECT on the window's header or border and drag the window to the new location. Press SELECT on any part of an icon to drag it to a new location.

  To move a window to the front of the screen, click SELECT on any part of the window header except the Window menu button. To move an icon to the front of the screen, click SELECT on the part of the icon you can see.

- Close a window:

  Convert a window to an icon (close a window) by clicking SELECT on the Window menu button in the upper left-hand corner of the window. (If you have changed the default on the Window menu, clicking SELECT will execute the default you have specified instead of the Close command. See "Changing Menu Defaults" in Chapter 4 for more information on this.)

- Select an object:

  The File Manager application uses the SELECT button as a means of designating an object on which you can perform file management commands.

- Operate a menu button or menu item:

  When you press SELECT on a menu button or item, a submenu comes up just as it does when you press MENU. You execute an item on the submenu by dragging to the item and releasing SELECT. Clicking SELECT will display the submenu without executing any of its items.

This function can be changed via the miscellaneous workspace property window. If you set the properties to execute the default item on a sub-menu, you will click SELECT on a menu button to execute the default of that button's submenu. You will press SELECT to display the default item without executing it. Refer to the section, "Miscellaneous Workspace Property Window," in Chapter 5 for information on changing this function.

The ADJUST Button

The ADJUST button is used with only some of the applications. In the File Manager application, it enables you to select several objects at once to perform a common function. For example, if you want to perform the same menu action on two or more objects, you can move the pointer to the first object and click SELECT. Then move the pointer to a second object and click ADJUST. This extends the selection. Do this with any number of objects until you are ready to make a choice from the menu. The ADJUST button also toggles the selected state of an entry, from selected to unselected and back again.

The MENU Button

The MENU button is used to display menus and select items on menus. The location of the pointer determines which menu is displayed; for example, if you press MENU when the pointer is in the workspace, the workspace menu is displayed.

There are two ways to use the mouse in order to view and choose from any menu:

- Press-Drag-Release
- Click-Move-Click

All procedures in this manual use the press-drag-release method for menu access, which results in the menu being displayed in the "pop-up" mode. See the section "Operating on Menus" in Chapter 4 for descriptions of the "pop-up" and "stay-up" modes of menus, and procedures for obtaining both.

Perform the following steps to access a menu with the press-drag-release method:

1. Press MENU. The menu that corresponds to the pointer location appears.

2. Continue to hold the MENU button down while dragging the pointer from menu item to menu item.

3. Once the pointer is on the item you want, release MENU. The action is initiated, and the menu is dismissed.

If you release MENU after you drag the pointer off the menu, the menu is dismissed and no action is initiated.

Using a One- or Two-Button Mouse

If your mouse has only one or two buttons instead of the recommended three, you can combine mouse buttons with keyboard keys (modifiers) to perform the same functions as shown in Figure 2-4. See the section, "Mouse Modifiers Workspace Property Window" in Chapter 5 for information about modifier keys and how to identify or change them.

Figure 2-4: Default Modifiers for One- or Two-Button Mouse

Function	One-Button	Two-Button
SELECT	Mouse button	Left button
ADJUST	Shift/Mouse button	Shift/Left button
MENU	CTRL/Mouse button	Right button

The Mouse Pointer

The mouse is "connected" electronically to a graphic symbol on your screen known as the pointer. As you move the mouse across the surface of your desk, the pointer moves similarly across your screen.

The symbol representing the pointer may look different depending on the application you are running. The table in Figure 2-5 illustrates the pointer as it appears in the OPEN LOOK Interface and the Terminal Emulator application.

Figure 2-5: Mouse Pointer Symbols

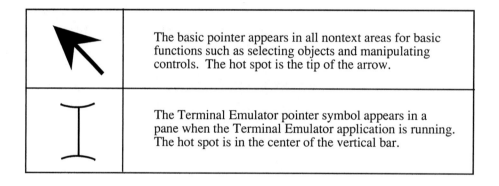

⬉	The basic pointer appears in all nontext areas for basic functions such as selecting objects and manipulating controls. The hot spot is the tip of the arrow.
⌶	The Terminal Emulator pointer symbol appears in a pane when the Terminal Emulator application is running. The hot spot is in the center of the vertical bar.

Pointer Jumping

You move the pointer by moving the mouse. However, an OPEN LOOK Interface application can occasionally move the pointer for you, by jumping it directly to a specific place on the screen, such as the elevator of a scroll bar.

Using the Keyboard

Instead of using the buttons on a mouse, you can use one of the following methods to perform the same procedure from the keyboard.

- Mnemonics

    Mnemonic functionality allows you to perform a function, such as accessing a submenu or menu item, by typing one or more keystrokes in sequence. Mnemonics will only perform properly if the window, control, or workspace you are in has active input focus. This means that the window must accept input from the keyboard or mouse. You can determine whether a window has active input focus by looking at the header of the window; if it is colored or highlighted, the window has active input focus. A button has active input focus if it is highlighted (2D mode) or if it looks "depressed" and is filled with the input focus color (3D mode).

    Since a mnemonic is defined within an active window, two menus can use the mnemonic "A," for example, but the menu with the input focus is the one that will be accessed when you press (a). Pressing (ALT) (F6) allows you to move the focus to a window. If none of the windows have active input focus, the system beeps when you try to enter information from the keyboard. See Chapter 4, "The OPEN LOOK Interface: Procedures," for more on active input focus.

    There are two ways to use mnemonics:

    - If you are within a menu, you can access the submenus listed by typing the appropriate mnemonic for that submenu. For example, as shown in Figure 2-6, if you press (p) while you are in the Workspace Menu, you will access the Programs submenu. This mnemonic is the equivalent of traversing to the menu and opening it with (F4). Notice that in Figure 2-6, each mnemonic is underlined. The Workspace Manager Property Sheets allow you to underline or highlight the mnemonics on your screen, or to turn the mnemonics display off completely, if you choose. You will learn more about this feature in Chapter 5, "The Workspace Manager Application."

Figure 2-6: The Workspace Menu

□ If you are not within a menu, but are within an application window, you must use a mnemonic prefix in combination with the mnemonic in order to access a button. The mnemonic prefix for OPEN LOOK is **ALT**.

If you are unsure of which mnemonic character to use in a specific instance, refer to the highlighted or underlined mnemonic characters displayed on the screen; mnemonics will automatically be underlined when you start the OPEN LOOK system.

 NOTE   Mnemonics should not be entered as uppercase characters, unless specified; lowercase letters are acceptable. Any printable character can be used as a mnemonic; do not use blank spaces.

■ Acceleration Acceleration allows you to access controls, menus, and sub-menus, using a combination of keystrokes. Unlike mnemonics, accelerators are global to an application and do not require active input focus in the window containing the control in order to operate (provided some window or control in the application has active input focus). In addition, the control does not even need to be visible. Therefore, even if the menu choice you want to access is not displayed on the screen as an option, you can use an accelerator to access it. For example, pressing **ALT** **F4**

allows you to quit an application without having to bring up the Window menu and selecting the Quit option from the menu. Like mnemonics, you can choose to turn the display of accelerators on or off.

Menu Navigation With the Keyboard

Keyboard Navigation

This feature allows you to select the active input area using the [TAB] or [CTRL] [TAB] and [SHIFT] [TAB] or [SHIFT] [CTRL] [TAB] navigation keys on the keyboard.

- The [SHIFT] [TAB] key moves the input focus to the previous menu item or control. If the input focus is on the first item of the menu, pressing [SHIFT] [TAB] will wrap to the last item of the menu.

- The [TAB] key moves the input focus to the next menu item. If the input focus is on the last item of the menu, then pressing [TAB] will wrap to the first item of the menu.

- The [ESC] key will unpost the menu and leave the input focus on the menu button.

- If input focus is on a menu button within a menu, pressing [CTRL] [m] will post the submenu associated with the menu button.

You can also use the following keys to move around and between windows.

- NEXTFIELD moves to the next control in the window; the system default is [TAB] or [CTRL] [TAB].

- PREVFIELD moves to the previous control in the window; the system default is [SHIFT] [TAB] or [SHIFT] [CTRL] [TAB].

  Both [CTRL] [TAB] and [SHIFT] [CTRL] [TAB] are used when the input focus is in a text field.

- NEXTWINDOW moves to the next window in the application; the system default is [ALT] [F6].

- PREVWINDOW moves to the previous window in the application; the system default is ⌈**SHIFT**⌉ ⌈**ALT**⌉ ⌈**F6**⌉.

- NEXTAPPLICATION moves to the first window in the next application; the system default is ⌈**ALT**⌉ ⌈**ESC**⌉.

- PREVAPPLICATION moves to the first window in the previous application; the system default is ⌈**SHIFT**⌉ ⌈**ALT**⌉ ⌈**ESC**⌉.

Once you have moved focus to the desired item, you can manipulate that item using the keyboard equivalents for the mouse buttons, shown below.

Table 2-1: Keyboard Equivalent Functions for Mouse Buttons

Use This Key	To Perform This Mouse Function
SPACEBAR or CTRL-SPACEBAR	SELECT
CTRL-&	ADJUST
CTRL-m or F4	MENU

OPEN LOOK Keyboard Commands and Their Physical Bindings

OPEN LOOK keys have specific keystrokes assigned to them. These keystroke assignments are called key bindings or key sequences and refer to the actual keys that you must press in order to perform the function that the OPEN LOOK key represents. For example, to perform the OPEN LOOK (MENUKEY) function, you would press (CTRL) (m) or (F4). In this guide, the default keystroke assignments are used, but you may change the settings for these keys (except for the system accelerators). To change or customize key bindings, you use the Property sheets. See Chapter 5, "The Workspace Manager Application," for more information.

The remainder of this section provides the default keystrokes for the various OPEN LOOK keyboard commands. You should keep these tables handy and refer to them whenever you use the keyboard to perform an OPEN LOOK function.

Table 2-2: Core Functions

Core Function Keys	
Function Key Name	Key Sequences
CUT	<SHIFT><DELETE>
COPY	<CTRL><INSERT>
PASTE	<SHIFT><INSERT>
UNDO	<ALT><BACKSPACE>
HELP	<f1>
PROPERTIES	<CTRL><p>
STOP	<CTRL><s>
DEFAULTACTION	<RETURN> or <CTRL><RETURN>
CANCEL	<ESC>

Table 2-3: Navigation Functions

Navigation Keys	
Function Key Name	Key Sequences
NEXTFIELD	<TAB> or <CTRL><TAB>
PREVFIELD	<SHIFT><TAB> or <SHIFT><CTRL><TAB>
UP	<UP ARROW>
DOWN	<DOWN ARROW>
LEFT	<LEFT ARROW>
RIGHT	<RIGHT ARROW>
NEXTWINDOW	<ALT><F6>
PREVWINDOW	<SHIFT><ALT><F6>
NEXTAPPLICATION	<ALT><ESC>
PREVAPPLICATION	<SHIFT><ALT><ESC>
WORDFWD	<CTRL><RIGHT ARROW>
WORDBACK	<CTRL><LEFT ARROW>
LINESTART	<HOME>
LINEEND	<END>
PANESTART	<SHIFT><CTRL><HOME>
PANEEND	<SHIFT><CTRL><END>
DOCSTART	<CTRL><HOME>
DOCEND	<CTRL><END>

Table 2-4: Text Edit Functions

Text Edit Functions	
Function Key Name	Key Sequences
DELCHARFWD	<DELETE>
DELCHARBACK	<BACKSPACE>
DELWORDFWD	<CTRL><SHIFT><DELETE>
DELWORDBACK	<CTRL><SHIFT><BACKSPACE>
DELLINEFWD	<CTRL><DELETE>
DELLINEBACK	<CTRL><BACKSPACE>
DELLINE	<ALT><SHIFT><DELETE>

Table 2-5: Scrolling Functions

Scrolling Functions	
Function Key Name	Key Sequences
SCROLLUP	<PAGE-UP>
SCROLLDOWN	<PAGE-DOWN>
SCROLLLEFT	<ALT>[
SCROLLRIGHT	<ALT>]
PAGEUP	<CTRL><PAGE-UP>
PAGEDOWN	<CTRL><PAGE-DOWN>
PAGELEFT	<CTRL>[
PAGERIGHT	<CTRL>]
SCROLLTOP	<ALT><PAGE-UP>
SCROLLBOTTOM	<ALT><PAGE-DOWN>
SCROLLEFTEDGE	<ALT><SHIFT> {
SCROLLRIGHTEDGE	<ALT><SHIFT> }

Table 2-6: Text Selection Functions

Text Selection Functions	
Function Key Name	Key Sequences
SELECTCHARFWD	<SHIFT><RIGHT>
SELECTWORDFWD	<SHIFT><CTRL><RIGHT>
SELECTLINEFWD	<SHIFT><END>
SELECTCHARBACK	<SHIFT><LEFT>
SELECTWORDBACK	<SHIFT><CTRL><LEFT>
SELECTLINEBACK	<SHIFT><HOME>
SELECTLINE	<CTRL><ALT><LEFT>
FLIPSELECTIONENDS	<ALT><INSERT>

Table 2-7: System Functions

System Functions	
Function Key Name	Key Sequences
TOGGLEPUSHPIN	<CTRL><t>
WORKSPACEMENU	<CTRL><w>
WINDOWMENU	<SHIFT><ESC>
SCROLLBARMENU (Vertical)	<CTRL><r>
SCROLLBARMENU (Horizontal)	<ALT><CTRL><r>
MNEMONICPREFIX	<ALT>

Keyboard and Mouse Specifications

All of the mouse button functions are available from the keyboard as well as from the mouse. Different applications may require keyboard strokes for some of their functions.

The keyboard settings workspace property window lists the default mappings for these functions. You can change the mappings for all keyboard functions from this property window. Information on the keyboard settings workspace property window is found in the subsection, "Keyboard Functions Workspace Property Window," in Chapter 5.

You can assign additional functionality by pressing a modifier key in conjunction with one of the mouse buttons. Use the mouse settings workspace property window to customize the mouse buttons in this way. See "Mouse Modifiers Workspace Property Window" in Chapter 5 for information on combining mouse button movements with modifier keys.

Using the OPEN LOOK Interface

This section provides step-by-step procedures for:

- Logging in
- Creating a window
- Running an application
- Closing a window and opening an icon
- Quitting an application from both an icon and window
- Quitting the OPEN LOOK Interface
- Configuring the Interface

Even if you have a color monitor, the OPEN LOOK environment is black and white when you first log in. The OPEN LOOK Interface has a wide range of colors available, and you can set these colors for all elements of your system if you have a color monitor. Refer to the section "Color Workspace Property Window" in Chapter 5 for information on setting colors.

If you plan to use the OPEN LOOK Interface only occasionally, you will type olinit when you log in. If you would like an automatic startup which will immediately put you in the OPEN LOOK environment, see the section "Miscellaneous Workspace Property Window" in Chapter 5.

Logging In

To use the OPEN LOOK Interface, you must be identified as an OPEN LOOK user. Your system administrator may have done this for you already. If you are identified to the system as an OPEN LOOK user, then you can access the OPEN LOOK Interface by doing the following:

1. Turn your computer on and enter your login ID and password.

2. At the UNIX System prompt (usually $), type:

   olinit

   and press (↵).

If you cannot access the OPEN LOOK Interface by typing olinit, it is probably because you have not been identified as an OPEN LOOK user to the system. Refer to "Adding a User" later in this chapter for information on adding yourself to the system.

When running across a network to a remote X server, type

olwsm&

at the UNIX System prompt and press (↵). When running the clients and server on the same machine, type olinit instead of olwsm&. If running on a 3B2, type olwsm&.

3. An X appears in the middle of the screen. Wait until the screen refreshes and the X turns into the basic pointer. When you hear a beep, this indicates that the OPEN LOOK Interface is ready.

You are now able to access the OPEN LOOK Interface workspace menu, as described in the next procedure, "Creating a Window." All OPEN LOOK client applications and applications installed by your site are available from the workspace menu. Chapters 3 and 4 will explain the workspace menu more thoroughly.

If you are not using a mouse to run OPEN LOOK, during initialization of the software, the message, "WARNING: Mouse driver not found; continuing" will be displayed and the initialization process will continue.

Creating a Window

To create a Terminal Emulator window, do the following:

1. When the system beeps to indicate that it is ready,

MOUSE: Press and hold down MENU, as described in "Using the Mouse." Do not release the MENU button.

KEYBD: Press (**CTRL**) (**w**).

A menu called the Workspace Menu appears on the screen as shown in Figure 2-7:

Figure 2-7: Getting Started: The OPEN LOOK Interface Workspace Menu

---

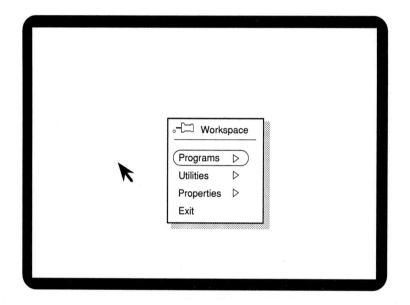

NOTE | If you ran `oladduser` first, the workspace menu will appear automatically at the top left corner of the screen upon startup. In this case, you do not have to use the mouse to bring up the workspace menu.

2. Access the Programs submenu.

    MOUSE: With the MENU button depressed, drag the pointer to the Programs label on the Workspace menu, and continue to drag to the triangular symbol to the right of the Programs label.

    KEYBD: Type ⎡**p**⎤.

A complete list of the mnemonic characters you can use in order to access each menu and submenu on the Workspace is provided in Chapter 5.

The label highlights and you will see a submenu which lists the application programs available from the workspace.

Figure 2-8: Getting Started: Programs Submenu

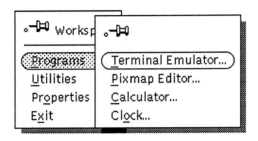

3. From the submenu,

MOUSE: Drag the pointer to the Terminal Emulator label on the submenu and release.

KEYBD: Type ⓣ.

(There may be several programs besides Terminal Emulator listed on your Programs submenu.)

A window similar to the following screen appears:

Figure 2-9: Getting Started: The Terminal Emulator Window

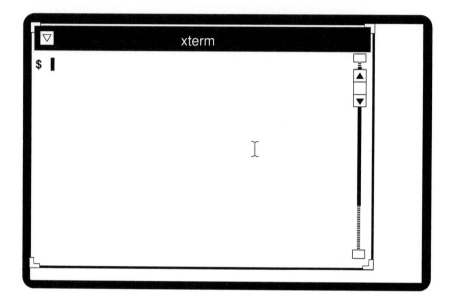

Running an Application

The Terminal Emulator window gives you a UNIX prompt and you can execute
UNIX commands from this window as long as the window has active input
focus. To run an application from the Terminal Emulator window, type the
command that starts the application at the UNIX System prompt, and press
⏎. See page 4 if you have to establish input focus in the window.

Running Multiple Applications

You can create as many Terminal Emulator windows as you want, and run one or more applications.

To create a second window, perform the following steps:

MOUSE:

1. Position the pointer in the workspace and press MENU.

2. Drag the pointer to Programs.

3. Continue to drag the pointer to Terminal Emulator on the submenu and release MENU.

KEYBD:

1. Press (CTRL) (w) to access the Workspace menu.

2. Type (p) to select the Programs option.

3. Type (t) to select the Terminal Emulator option.

Another window labeled "Terminal Emulator," identical to the first one, appears on the workspace. It partly hides the first window. The new window has the active input focus.

Running the ico Application

The application in the following example is ico, a common X application. This application creates an animated polyhedron.

1. Create a window as described in the subsection, "Creating a Window."

2. Type

```
ico &
```

at the UNIX System prompt and press (↵). The following *ico* window appears:

Figure 2-10: Getting Started: Running an Application

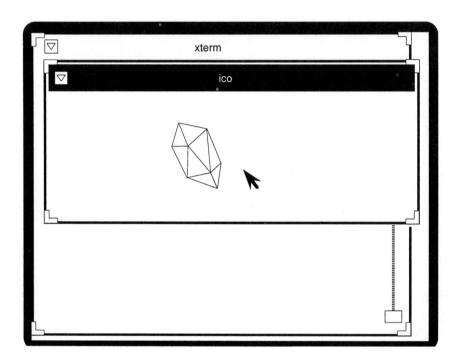

Closing a Window

Closing a window converts it to an icon, in which the program, or application, continues to run, but is out of the way while you work on other windows.

Use the following procedure to close or "iconify" a window.

MOUSE:

1. Position the pointer in the top portion (the header) of the ico window directly below the border of the window.

2. Press MENU.

3. Drag the pointer to Close.

4. Release MENU.

KEYBD:

1. If the window does not have input focus, press (ALT) (ESC) to move input focus to the window; if necessary, press (ALT) (F6) to move focus to a window within an application.

2. Press (SHIFT) (ESC).

   A list of window options appears.

3. Type (c) or (ALT) (F5).

   — or —

   If the window has input focus, you can close it simply by typing (ALT) (F5).

As the window becomes an icon, lines radiate from it, to show where it will be placed. It is reduced to a small square and moves to the workspace, where it runs in the background until you open it again.

Opening an Icon

You can "open" the icon to return it to its window size.

MOUSE:

1. Move the pointer to the icon and press MENU.

2. Release MENU on Open.

KEYBD:

1. If the icon does not have input focus, press (**ALT**) (**ESC**) to move input focus to the window.

2. Press (**SHIFT**) (**ESC**)

   A list of window options appears.

3. Type (**o**) or (**ALT**) (**F5**).

   — or —

   If the icon has input focus, you can open it simply by typing (**ALT**) (**F5**).

Lines radiate from the icon and it enlarges once again to become a window.

Quitting an Application

You can quit an application from either the icon or window state. These procedures quit the application only, not the entire OPEN LOOK system.

Quitting From an Icon

Follow these steps to quit from an icon

MOUSE:

1. Move the pointer to the icon.

2. Press MENU.

3. Drag the pointer to Quit and release.

KEYBD:

1. If the icon does not have input focus, press (**ALT**) (**ESC**) to move input focus to the window.

2. Press (**SHIFT**) (**ESC**).

   A list of window options appears.

3. Type $\boxed{\text{q}}$ or $\boxed{\textbf{ALT}}$ $\boxed{\textbf{F4}}$.

— or —

If the icon has input focus, you can quit simply by typing $\boxed{\textbf{ALT}}$ $\boxed{\textbf{F4}}$.

Quitting From a Window

MOUSE:

1. Move the pointer to the top portion (the header) of the window.

2. Press MENU.

3. Drag the pointer to Quit and release.

KEYBD:

1. If the window does not have input focus, press $\boxed{\textbf{ALT}}$ $\boxed{\textbf{ESC}}$ to move input focus to the window.

2. Press $\boxed{\textbf{SHIFT}}$ $\boxed{\textbf{ESC}}$.

3. Type $\boxed{\text{q}}$ or $\boxed{\textbf{ALT}}$ $\boxed{\textbf{F4}}$.

— or —

If the window has input focus, you can quit simply by typing $\boxed{\textbf{ALT}}$ $\boxed{\textbf{F4}}$.

Quitting the OPEN LOOK Interface

This procedure exits the systems and shuts down every application currently running. You should first quit from any windows running, however you can still exit OPEN LOOK without quitting currently running applications.

Follow these steps to exit the system:

MOUSE:

1. Move the pointer to the workspace.

2. Press MENU .

3. Drag the pointer to Exit and release MENU.

   A notice box appears with the query, "Do you want to exit all running programs and the workspace?"

4. Move the pointer to Yes and click SELECT.

   All running applications are terminated and you return to the UNIX System prompt.

KEYBD:

1. Press (CTRL) (w) to access the Workspace Menu.

2. Type (x) to exit.

   A notice box appears with the query, "Do you want to exit all running programs and the workspace?"

3. Use the (←) or (→) keys to move the input focus to the button labeled
   Yes and press (↵).

   — or —

   Press (ALT) (y) to select Yes.

   All running applications are terminated and you return to the UNIX System prompt.

Configuration Procedures

If you have system administrator privileges, you can log in as root and use the programs described in this section to customize the user environment. root can add users to the OPEN LOOK Interface, remove users, and change the user environment for any user of the OPEN LOOK Interface. If you do not have root privileges, you can still use all of the programs described in this section, but are restricted to customizing your own environment.

This section describes the use of the following commands for user administration.

- oladduser. This program sets up a user's login environment.

- olremuser. This program undoes the user environment established by oladduser.

- olsetvar. This program sets certain shell variables used by the OPEN LOOK Interface system.

 While some of the files described in this chapter can be customized, files not mentioned at all should not be tampered with by any user. In particular, users should be warned against modifying their .olprograms file. Any login or resource added to this file will be treated as a program and added to the scrolling list in the programs submenu workspace property window. Changes of any kind should be made via the workspace property windows.

Adding a User

All users on the OPEN LOOK system have to be identified to the system before they can have login privileges. The oladduser command must be executed one time for each user. The system administrator can add any user, or a user can add him or herself.

New OPEN LOOK users must already have UNIX System login IDs and a .profile file.

1. Type the following to add a user:

    # /usr/X/adm/oladduser *<login_id>*

   oladduser adds the following line to the user's *.profile:*

   . $HOME/.olsetup <TAB> #!@ Do not edit this line @

2. The following six files will be added to the user's home directory:

   ■ .olsetup. This file is executed upon login to start the olinit
   process and check the value of the variables to decide whether to
   start up the OPEN LOOK Interface automatically. You should
   not touch this file. Automatic startup is set via the miscellaneous
   workspace property window. Refer to the section "Miscellaneous Workspace Property Window" in Chapter 5 for information
   on the miscellaneous workspace property window.

   ■ .Xdefaults. This file defines the values for OPEN LOOK
   Interface resources. It includes the values for two Terminal Emulator attributes: xterm*font and xterm*boldFont. Changes
   made via the workspace property windows will be reflected in
   the .Xdefaults file. Refer to the Xterm manual page in Appendix A for more information on these attributes.

   The inexperienced user should not tamper with the data in the
   .Xdefaults file. Changing or adding new resources can result in
   distortion of all the applications.

   ■ .olinitrc. This file is read by olinit to start up other OPEN
   LOOK applications.

   ■ .oliniterr. This file stores error messages. You should period-
   ically remove this file when it gets too big.

   ■ .olinitout. This file stores system messages from commands
   executed from the Workspace Manager.

   ■ .olprograms. This file contains information for the programs
   listed under Programs on the workspace property menu. Do not
   change or add to this file. Any login or resource added to this
   file will be treated as a program, and added to the scrolling list
   in the programs submenu property window. Any such changes
   should be made via the programs submenu workspace property
   window.

If the user is already an OPEN LOOK user, `oladduser` will overwrite all previous files except `.Xdefaults`. It will rename the file `.Xdefaults-old` and create a new `.Xdefaults` file. You may remove `.Xdefaults-old` if you have no need to refer to the information contained in it.

If the login is not valid, an error message is displayed.

Customizing the .olinitrc File

The `.olinitrc` file contains commands to run the Window Manager and File Manager applications. If you would like the Terminal Emulator application to come up automatically (before you invoke the workspace menu) when you log into the OPEN LOOK Interface, `cd` to your home directory and edit `.olinitrc` with the editor of your choice. Add the line `xterm &` to the end of the `.olinitrc` file.

You can remove the line `olfm &` from `.olinitrc` if you do not wish to run the File Manager application from the OPEN LOOK Interface. Removing `olfm` may increase system performance. Instead, you can invoke the File Manager application from the UNIX System prompt, by accessing a Terminal Emulator window and typing `nohup olfm &` at the UNIX System prompt. You can then use the workspace menu to access the File Manager application.

Removing a User

To remove a user from the OPEN LOOK Interface system, type the following:

```
# /usr/X/adm/olremuser <login_id>
```

The command removes the files added by `oladduser` from the user's home directory and removes the line

```
. $HOME/.olsetup <TAB>  #!@ Do not edit this line @
```

from the user's `.profile` file.

If you have a `.Xdefaults-old` file resulting from a previous installation of OPEN LOOK, that file will be automatically renamed `.Xdefaults` once again. You may remove it again with `olremuser`, in which case you will see a message

```
.Xdefaults will be removed.
```

olsetvar

It is possible to use the olsetvar program to set four shell variables used by the OPEN LOOK Interface. Refer to the manual pages in Appendix A for the syntax of olsetvar. The values of the variables are explained in the following table:

Figure 2-11: Setting Shell Variables with olsetvar

Variable	Values	Purpose
OLINVOKE	yes or no	To cause the OPEN LOOK Interface to start up automatically upon login. The default is no. This feature is normally set from the miscellaneous workspace property window. However, it is possible to set $OLINVOKE to yes to cause the OPEN LOOK Interface to start automatically upon login. Use /usr/X/adm/olsetvar OLINVOKE yes.
XNETACCESS	on or off	Security feature which allows other xhosts to connect to your machine. If you wish to maintain security, you can prevent your machine from connecting with others by setting this to on. The default is on.
PATH	string such as $PATH:/usr/X/bin	To append a directory string to your PATH variable.
DISPLAY	string such as unix:0	To specify a string for the X server.

3 THE OPEN LOOK Interface: Features

Introduction

The OPEN LOOK Graphical User Interface is a powerful system with a vast array of features. The OPEN LOOK Interface has been designed to support applications ranging from simple utilities to complex integrated applications, with features and functions that enable you to work smoothly and efficiently in many environments.

This chapter describes the windows and menus that comprise the OPEN LOOK Interface. Once you have familiarized yourself with the material in this chapter, go to Chapter 4 for step-by-step procedures for working with windows and menus.

Overview

The Window Manager application executes most of the functions that control the windows that are integral to the OPEN LOOK Interface. The Window Manager enables you to change the sizes of windows, convert windows into icons and icons into windows, and display their accompanying menus.

The Workspace Manager application helps the system manage the applications and execute programs. This application provides the workspace property windows, which make global changes to OPEN LOOK applications.

You will probably be unaware of any separation between the Window Manager, Workspace Manager, or any other application. The OPEN LOOK Interface provides a common look for all the applications.

This chapter is intended for the inexperienced user, assuming limited previous experience with the UNIX System or a windowing system, and does not use technical concepts or vocabulary.

If you want to use the features as you read about them in this chapter, you can use the mouse and its SELECT, ADJUST, and MENU buttons; you can also use the keys on the keyboard to use these features.

Procedures for using the mouse and keyboard to perform basic tasks are found in the sections "Using the Mouse," "Using the Keyboard," and "Using the OPEN LOOK Interface" in Chapter 2.

Organization of the Chapter

The contents of this chapter are arranged as follows:

- Windows and Icons

  Describes elements of the base window, pop-up windows, and icons.

- Controls

  Describes buttons and other controls, and placement and use of control areas.

- Menus

  Lists the different types of menus and their elements.

Windows and Icons

The OPEN LOOK window environment consists of the workspace and the windows, icons, and menus on the workspace. Figure 3-1 shows windows and icons in the workspace.

Figure 3-1: The OPEN LOOK Interface Base Window with Icons in the Workspace

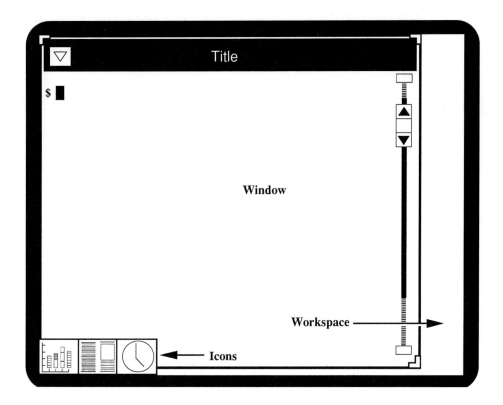

The workspace is the background screen area on which windows, menus, and icons appear. It is called a workspace to encourage you to think of the computer screen as a convenient work area, not unlike the desk at which you sit. In certain respects, you can treat the workspace as you would the surface of a desk or bulletin board. You can move windows and icons around the workspace, stack windows on top of each other like piles of papers, or use a "pushpin" to keep a window up on the screen. The workspace has its own menu, from which you perform activities that manage OPEN LOOK applications and utilities.

An OPEN LOOK window is identified by the border that frames it to distinguish it from the workspace. The OPEN LOOK Interface has two different types of windows: base windows and pop-up windows.

The Base Window

A base window is a rectangular work area on the workspace in which an application's contents, including text and graphics, are displayed.

Base Window Elements

All base windows contain the following elements:

- Border

  The border is the outline that surrounds the window to set it off from the workspace.

- Header

  The header is the strip that spans the top portion of the window. This space is reserved for the title of the application that is currently running. The title appears in the center of the header. The header may also contain a window menu mark or a pushpin.

- Title

  The application title appears in the center of the header, if the window is big enough. If the application does not provide a title, it defaults to the name of the application.

- Window Menu

  The window menu is invoked by pressing MENU on either the window menu button or anywhere on the window header; you can also invoke this menu by pressing the Window Menu accelerator key sequence. See Chapter 4, "The Open Look Interface: Procedures," for more information. This menu provides a list of selections that control characteristics of the base window. See page 30 for information about the window menu.

■ Window Menu Button

The window menu button is a small square button with an inverted triangle that appears in the header to the left of the title. This button invokes the window menu, or, if you use the shortcut operation of clicking SELECT, invokes the window menu default.

In addition, all base windows have one or both of the following:

■ Control Area

A control area is a region within a window, excluding the header and footer, that contains controls such as buttons, settings, check boxes, and sliders. An application might have a single control area at the top of the window, or several control areas, arranged horizontally or vertically. Typically, a base window will have one control area at the top, with the pane beneath it.

■ Pane

The pane is the area of the base window other than the control area, header, and footer, where all data pertaining to the currently running application is displayed and manipulated. An application may have multiple panes within the same base window.

Figure 3-2 shows some of the required and optional elements of the base window.

Figure 3-2: The Base Window

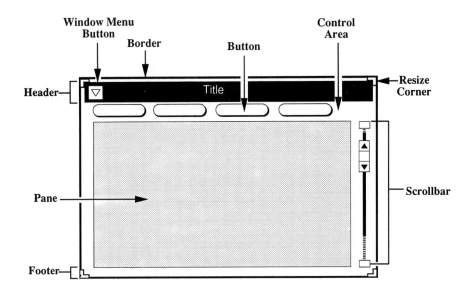

Optional Elements

The following elements are supplied if required by the application. Not all applications provide these features.

- Footer

  The footer is the space that spans the bottom portion of the window. The footer displays messages issued by the application.

- Resize Corners

  Resize corners enable you to make a window larger or smaller by dragging on the corner while pressing SELECT.

■ Scrollbar

Scrollbars are used to move text or graphics vertically or horizontally within a window, making it possible for you to look at text or graphics that otherwise do not fit within the window. You drag the scrollbar up or down or to the left or right to move the information on the screen and display previously hidden information.

Multiple Base Windows

While most applications have only one base window, more complex applications may have several. Each base window that forms its own window group is independent and has its own icon.

Pop-Up Windows

Pop-up windows appear in order to accomplish a specific purpose and are usually dismissed once that purpose is met. The OPEN LOOK pop-up windows include:

■ Command windows

■ Property windows

The window menus on command windows and property windows differ slightly from the base window menu. See page 32 for information on pop-up window menus.

The pushpin is a mandatory feature of command windows and property windows. It appears to the left side of the header.

Pushpins

Pushpins allow you to keep a pop-up window on display for as long as you want to refer to it and to dismiss it without using the pop-up window menu. Normally, when you execute a command or apply changes to a property window, an unpinned window is dismissed once the action is executed. A pinned window remains on screen even after execution of the command.

Dismiss all pop-up windows by clicking SELECT twice on the pushpin (once to pin it, and a second time to unpin it). Command windows and property windows can be pinned until you are ready to dismiss them, or can be used and dismissed without pinning.

Figure 3-3 shows the pushpin in a pinned and unpinned state.

Figure 3-3: A Pinned and Unpinned Window

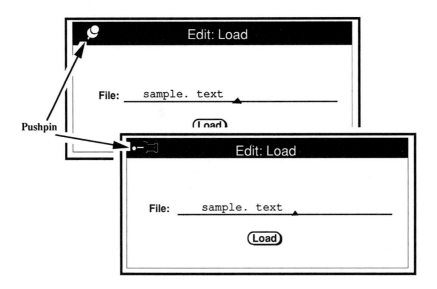

Menus can also have pushpins. A pinned menu loses its menu characteristics and becomes a pop-up command window with all the attributes and functionality of a command window: the title, pushpin, and pop-up window menu.

Command Windows

A command window is any window that enables you to perform a command function. Required elements of a command window are border, header, window menu, and pushpin. Optional elements are resize corners and a footer with message area. All command windows have the application title followed by the function of the command window. For example, the title of a File Manager application command window that copies files and directories is "File Manager: Copy."

Figure 3-4 shows a sample command window.

Figure 3-4: Command Window

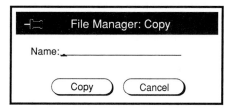

You can move a command window around by pressing SELECT anywhere on the window border or the header area (except on the pushpin) and dragging it to a new location. The next time you access the window, it will pop up in the new location. However, if you quit from the application, all command windows return to their application-defined position.

Property Windows

A property window is any window that enables you to set or change application-controlled characteristics, called properties. Figure 3-5 shows a property window.

Figure 3-5: Property Window

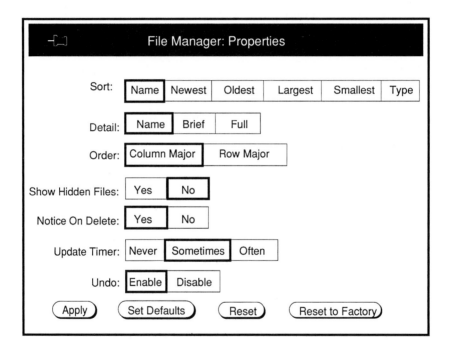

Property windows have the same elements as a command window, and has any or all of the following controls:

- Apply button

  Apply permanently sets all changed properties.

- Reset button

  Reset returns the property window settings to the current state of the selected object.

- Set Menu Defaults button

  Set Menu Defaults stores the applied settings to be used in subsequent base windows of the current application.

- Reset to Factory button

  Reset to Factory causes the properties of the window or application to return to the settings originally provided by the system.

You access a property window by selecting Properties from a menu.

The Workspace Property Windows

The workspace property windows, accessed from the workspace menu, are used to set global preferences, affecting all of the OPEN LOOK Interface rather than only one application. (Applications properties are set from the individual base windows, each of which has its own property window.)

There are six workspace property windows available when you select Properties from the workspace menu. The workspace property windows change properties for programs, icons, color, mouse settings, keyboard settings, and miscellaneous. Refer to Chapter 5 for information on the workspace property windows.

Icons

An icon is a small graphic symbol in a square border, that represents the application running in a window. You create an icon by "closing" a window. The window becomes reduced and moves to the workspace, where the application, or program, continues to run. This enables you to keep one program running and out of the way while you work on another, as shown in Figure 3-6.

Figure 3-6: Windows and Icons

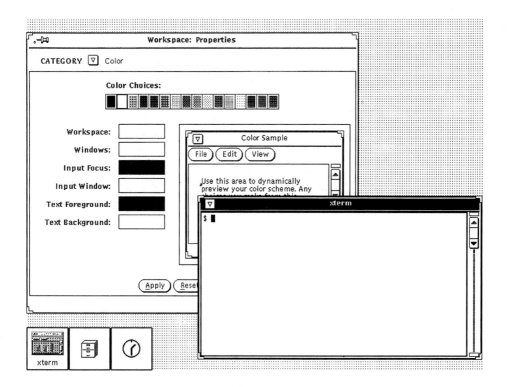

You close a window to convert it into an icon, and open the icon to convert it back into a window. The Close and Open commands are on the window menu, described on page 30.

An icon might be a graph to represent a graphics program, a drawing of a page to represent a word processing program, or simply the application title within a border. The Window Manager will provide a default icon image for applications that do not provide their own. Figure 3-7 shows examples of icons for the File Manager application and the xclock application.

Figure 3-7: Examples of Typical OPEN LOOK Interface Icons

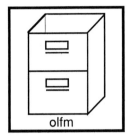

Default Icon Region

Windows that are converted into icons move to a default icon region at the bottom of the workspace. You can change the default icon region from the workspace property windows. See page 5-6 for information on changing the default icon region.

Icons might overlap when icon positioning is changed back to a previous setting or to one that starts at the same location as another setting. This can cause one icon to hide another.

In order minimize covering icons, avoid changing icon placement while icons are on the screen.

Controls

Controls are the buttons, items, and other features that appear on windows and menus to enable you to interact with applications. Although controls in a window are not necessarily grouped on the same side of the pane, the usual window has a control area at the top and a pane beneath, as shown in Figure 3-8.

Figure 3-8: A Control Area Above a Pane

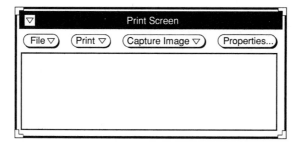

The OPEN LOOK Interface uses the following types of controls:

- Button controls (found on windows only)
- Check boxes (found on windows only)
- Menu items (found on menus only. See "Items on a Menu," starting on page 24, for information.)
- Settings (found on windows and menus)
- Sliders (found on windows only)
- Text fields (found on windows only)

The entire window can also be a control area. This is most likely to occur in command windows that pop up to perform specific functions. When the entire window is a control area, the controls are displayed within the pane.

Button Controls

Buttons are the most common type of control. They execute a single command or set parameters. The label on the button is the name of the function being executed. You click SELECT on a button to execute the function or you use the ⌜TAB⌟, and ⌜SHIFT⌟ ⌜TAB⌟ keys on the keyboard to move to the button; when you press ⌜spacebar⌟, you activate that control. You will see the following types of buttons on a control area:

■ Command button

■ Window button

■ Menu button

■ Abbreviated menu button

Command Button

A command button is used for a single command or function. Its label defines the function to be executed. For example, the "Apply" button in Figure 3-6 performs only that command and there are no associated menus or windows when you select it. To execute the command on a button's label, you click SELECT on the button or use the ⌜TAB⌟ and ⌜SHIFT⌟ ⌜TAB⌟ keys to move to the button and then press ⌜spacebar⌟.

Window Button

A window button is a button with an ellipsis (. . .) to the right of the button name. When you select a button with an ellipsis, you get a pop-up window. (See page 7 for information about pop-up windows.)

Figure 3-9: Window Buttons

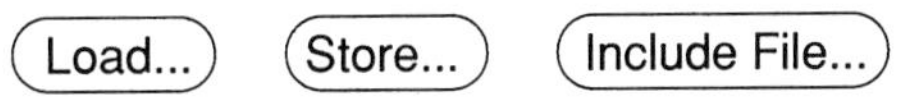

(Load...)   (Store...)   (Include File...)

Menu Button

A menu button designates a set or a group of related commands, which appear in the form of a submenu. A menu button is recognizable by the triangular arrow to the right of the label. The arrow points in the direction the submenu will appear when you select the button. You press or click MENU on the menu button to display the submenu; if you are using a keyboard, you will press [CTRL] [m].

Figure 3-10: Menu Buttons

Abbreviated Menu Button

Abbreviated menu buttons have a triangular arrow and function exactly like menu buttons, but are smaller and have no label. These small square buttons are used to save space, especially in windows. Figure 3-11 shows an abbreviated menu button.

Figure 3-11: Abbreviated Menu Button

 NOTE You can also access a submenu or its default item by using the SELECT mouse button on the menu button or abbreviated menu button. See "Miscellaneous Workspace Property Window" in Chapter 5 for information on this.

Visual Feedback

The visual feedback for each button depends on the conditions as described below:

- When the pointer is on a button and you press SELECT or ⟨**spacebar**⟩, the button is selected.

- When the pointer is on a menu button and you press MENU or ⟨**CTRL**⟩ ⟨**m**⟩, the menu button is selected.

- When a button cannot execute a command, the button outline and label are dimmed.

- When a button cannot accept input because it is busy responding to a requested action, the button background shows a busy pattern. Mouse clicks are ignored and an inappropriate keystroke will result in beeps.

- When you traverse to a button with the keyboard, it indicates that it is the current control by filling the interior of the button with the input focus color.

Figure 3-12 shows the different visual states of a button.

Figure 3-12: Button Visual Feedback

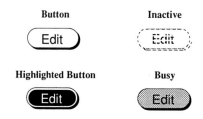

Check Boxes

Check boxes, shown in Figure 3-13 are a kind of nonexclusive setting provided
for lists of items that have a yes/no or on/off response. Check boxes are not
used in menus.

Move the pointer to the check box and click SELECT to toggle between the
checked and unchecked state.

Figure 3-13: Check Boxes and Labels

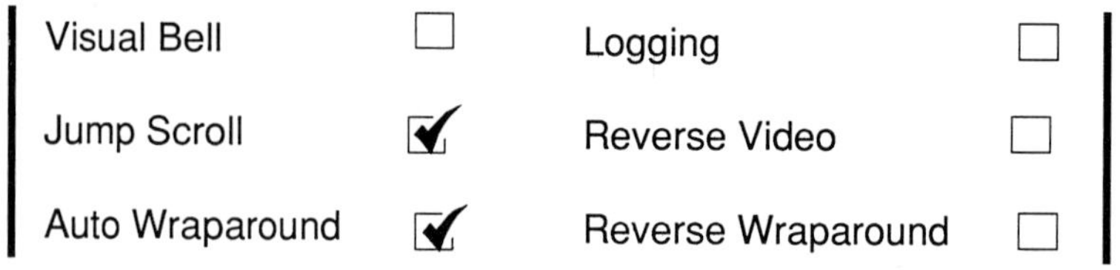

Visual Bell	□	Logging	□
Jump Scroll	☑	Reverse Video	□
Auto Wraparound	☑	Reverse Wraparound	□

Settings

Exclusive Settings

Exclusive settings are lists of choices from which you can make only one choice, and are shown as rectangles with touching borders. They are used when the object can be changed in some way, but changed to only one thing, such as the color of an object. You choose a setting by positioning the pointer in one of the rectangles and clicking SELECT. If you are using a keyboard, use the ⬆, ⬇, ➡, and ⬅ keys to move between settings. Use [**spacebar**] to choose the setting. The setting currently in use is displayed with a thicker, solid border. Exclusive settings can be used in combination with other controls, and as items on a submenu.

Figure 3-14 shows an example of an exclusive setting.

Figure 3-14: Exclusive Settings

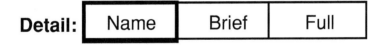

Nonexclusive Settings

Nonexclusive settings are used to set multiple values for the same object, such as the example in Figure 3-15 on which both the "Read" and "Execute" attributes were selected. Nonexclusive settings are displayed as separate rectangles. You can select all, none, or any combination of nonexclusive settings for the same object.

Figure 3-15: Nonexclusive Settings

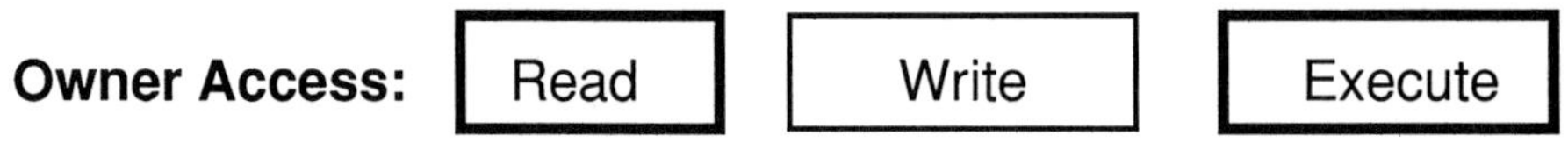

Owner Access:
Read
Write
Execute

Sliders

A slider is used to set a numeric value and give a visual indication of the setting. Sliders can be horizontal or vertical, as shown in Figure 3-16.

Figure 3-16: Sliders

0
100
with min/max values
100
0

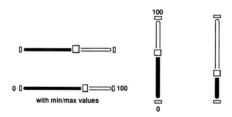

Text Fields

Text fields are used when the application requires keyboard input. A text field can appear in either a control area or pane, wherever the application requires you to type in some text.

You cannot type in a text field unless you give the field active input focus. Without it, your keystrokes will go to the control that has the active input focus. See the subsection "Using Text Fields" in Chapter 4 for information on typing in a text field.

Validating Text Fields

An application may check the information in a text field to ensure that it contains data an application can use. The application determines whether or not to validate a given text field.

Arrow Buttons in Text Fields

Text fields have a fixed length, although you may type more characters than the length of the field. When the field contains more text than it can show, arrow buttons are displayed at the beginning and/or end of the line to show that there are more characters in the direction shown by the arrow. Text fields should be long enough that display arrows are not needed for normal operation.

Figure 3-17 shows how the arrow buttons function. Note that this field is not long enough if "ABCDEF" is a value expected in normal operation.

Figure 3-17: A Text Field with Horizontal Scrolling Buttons

Name: _____ ABCD ▲_   Type characters in a four-character
                        field

Name: ◀DEF ▲_   When you type more characters,
                        (E and F in this example), the
                        first character of the field is
                        replaced by an arrow to
                        show that the field contains
                        more characters to the left.

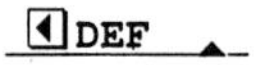

Name: ◀CD▲▶   If you click SELECT on the
                        left arrow, the text scrolls
                        one character to the right,
                        and an arrow is displayed at
                        the right of the field to
                        show that the field also
                        contains more characters to
                        the right.

Messages

There are two kinds of messages:

The first kind refers to read-only messages in panes, footers, or control areas, such as the titles or identifier for controls.

The second kind of message is used as a prompt to perform an action or to give status information. It can appear in any part of the window. Important messages, such as error messages, may be displayed in the footer and cause the system to beep.

Menus

Each region of the screen in the OPEN LOOK Interface has a menu. Menus provide additional control areas that are hidden from view until you need to use them.

The menu displayed on any window or workspace area is identified according to its source — when the pointer is on the workspace and you press MENU, the workspace menu is displayed. When the pointer is on a scrollbar and you press MENU, a scrollbar menu is displayed.

Required Menus

The OPEN LOOK Interface provides the following menus:

- Workspace menu
- Window menu
- Pop-up window menu
- Settings menu for property window panes
- Scrollbar menu

Individual applications may use menus that are defined by the application, such as the xterm menus, described in Chapter 7.

Menu Elements

A menu is a rectangular form, identified by the drop shadow in three-dimensional look. A menu has at least two choices, in the form of menu items and/or settings. Most of the menus in the OPEN LOOK Interface consist of a vertical row of items, but a menu can also be made up of exclusive or nonexclusive settings as described on page 19. There is only one default choice per menu. The default item is identifiable by the ring around it that gives it the form of a button. The pushpin can also be the default with the ring around it. As each item is selected on the menu, it highlights by also changing to a button shape and reversing its color.

An optional menu element is the pushpin. A menu pushpin works like the window pushpin already described, by pinning a menu to the workspace or window. However, a pinned menu takes on the characteristics of a command window. Although the menu items do not develop the outlines of buttons, the pinned menu acquires all other attributes and functionality of a command window, and can be moved and manipulated with a popup window menu. See page 7 for information about pushpins.

Items on a Menu

Menu items correspond in functionality to buttons. One or more of the following items can be found on a menu:

- Command item

- Menu item

- Window item

One menu item will be the default. Figure 3-18, below, shows a typical menu with two different types of menu items. "Programs" is the default, indicated by the button-shaped ring around the label.

Figure 3-18: Items on a Menu

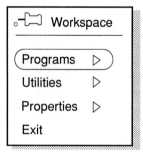

Command Item

A command item, like a command button, executes a single command. It consists of a simple label; for example, "Exit" in Figure 3-18 exits the workspace. Click SELECT on the item to execute the command.

Menu Item

A menu item designates a set or a group of related commands, which appear in the form of a submenu. A submenu is the more detailed menu that appears when you select a menu item on a menu. A menu item has a triangular arrow to the right of the label. The arrow points to the right, in the direction the submenu will appear when you select the item. Programs, Utilities, and Properties in Figure 3-18 are all menu items.

Press or click MENU on the menu item to display the submenu or use keyboard traversal to move focus to the menu item and press ⌈**CTRL**⌋ ⌈**m**⌋.

 NOTE You can also access a submenu or its default item by using the SELECT mouse button on the menu button or abbreviated menu button. See "Miscellaneous Workspace Property Window" in Chapter 5 for information on this.

Window Item

Selection of a window item produces an associated pop-up window. The ellipsis (. . .) appearing after the label identifies this as a window item. The Accepted Remote Hosts and Outgoing Remote Displays labels in Figure 3-19 are examples of window items. Click SELECT on the window item to bring up the pop-up window or move focus to the window item and press ⌈**spacebar**⌋.

Menu Default

The default choice on any menu is identified by the button-like outline, as shown on the Programs item on the workspace menu in Figure 3-18. The default choice is the item to which the cursor jumps when the menu is invoked.

You can change the setting on the miscellaneous workspace property window so that the menu default is the item executed if you click SELECT instead of MENU on a menu button or menu item.

For example, to select the default without going through the steps of pressing MENU and then clicking SELECT on the item, you would click SELECT on the Programs item on the workspace property menu. The default is executed (in this case, the Terminal Emulator window appears) and you never even see the Programs submenu. This setting would let you click SELECT on any menu button or menu item to execute the default item for that associated menu or submenu. Similarly, when you are using the keyboard with this option, the $\boxed{\hookleftarrow}$ key will execute the default.

Of course, you should know what to expect if you choose to execute the default in this way, but repeated use of a menu will familiarize you with the selections. (You can preview the default selection by pressing SELECT and holding it and then moving off the highlighted item; you cannot preview the selection if you are using a keyboard.) You can change the default choice on any menu or submenu. See "Changing Menu Defaults" in Chapter 4 for information on changing the default. Refer to "Miscellaneous Workspace Property Window" for information on changing "SELECT Mouse Press" in order to automatically execute the default.

Menu Group

Any menu together with its submenus is called a menu group. Figure 3-19 shows an example of a menu group which comes from the Utilities menu item on the workspace menu.

Figure 3-19: Menu Group with Two Submenus

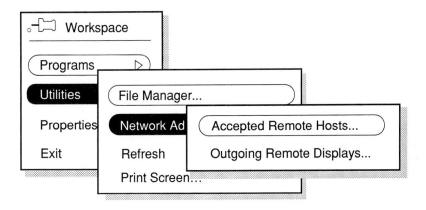

NOTE | The example above reflects the Network submenu for OPEN LOOK GUI running on SVR3.2.x. On SVR4.0, the Network Administration submenu is not displayed. Instead, selecting the Network Administration button will bring up the Accepted Remote Hosts window.

The Utilities menu item invokes a submenu with the choices of File Manager, Network Administration, Refresh, and Print Screen. The Network Manager menu item in turn invokes another submenu with two window items, Accepted Remote Hosts and Outgoing Remote Displays.

Workspace Menu

The workspace menu gives you access to all programs and properties for the OPEN LOOK Interface. No matter what application or window you are working in, you can always invoke the workspace menu by moving the pointer out of the application you are in and onto the workspace (the area surrounding the window). Press or click MENU. If you are using a keyboard, press CTRL w to invoke the Workspace Menu.

If you are using a keyboard and want to select a submenu from the Workspace Menu, type the related mnemonic character, as shown below.

- Programs. $\boxed{\text{p}}$

- Utilities. $\boxed{\text{u}}$

- Properties. $\boxed{\text{o}}$

- Exit. $\boxed{\text{x}}$

Figure 3-20: The Workspace Menu

The workspace menu, shown in Figure 3-20, has the following elements in addition to the standard menu elements:

- Title: Workspace

- Pushpin

- Programs

    The Programs menu item displays a submenu with a list of application programs that can be run from the workspace. (See Chapter 5 for details on adding programs to this submenu.)

Terminal Emulator is the default item on the Programs submenu. See Chapter 7 for more information on the Terminal Emulator application. Other program names depend on what programs are available at your site.

■ Utilities

The Utilities menu item accesses a submenu with the following choices:

☐ File Manager. Select this item for the File Manager application, described in Chapter 6.

☐ Network Administration. Select this item for the Administration Manager application, described in Chapter 8.

☐ Refresh. This redisplays all windows on the workspace.

☐ Print Screen. Select this item for the Print Screen window, described in Chapter 9.

To access the Utilities submenus from the keyboard, use one of the following mnemonics:

Print Screen. (**p**)

File Manager. (**f**)

Refresh. (**r**)

Network Administration. (**n**)

■ Properties. The Properties menu item accesses a submenu with the following window items:

☐ Programs Submenu

☐ Icons

☐ Color

☐ Mouse Modifiers

☐ Mouse Settings

□ Keyboard Functions

□ Miscellaneous

Each one of these window items invokes a property window from which you can change the specified settings. To access the Properties submenus from the keyboard, use the following mnemonics:

Programs. (p)

Icons. (i)

Color. (c)

Mouse Modifiers. (o)

Mouse Settings. (s)

Keyboard Functions. (k)

Miscellaneous. (m)

See Chapter 5 for more information on the Workspace Property windows.

■ Exit.

The Exit command item quits all elements of the workspace and any applications currently running. When you select Exit, a notice is displayed that reads, "Do you want to exit all running programs and the workspace?" You click SELECT on Yes (to continue with the exit), or No (to cancel the action). You must select one of the buttons in order to proceed.

Window Menu

You get a window menu whenever you press MENU on a base window header or on an icon created from a base window. You also get this menu when you press (SHIFT) (ESCAPE). The menu will appear near the header of the window that currently has input focus.

Figure 3-21: The Window Menu

The window menu, shown in Figure 3-21, has the following elements in addition to standard menu elements:

■ Title: Window

■ Open/Close

Either Open or Close appears as the command item, depending on whether the menu is accessed from a window or an icon.

The label toggles between Open and Close in the following way: if the window menu is accessed from a window, the label reads "Close." This is because the window is already open, and the only function of the two you can perform is to close it. If accessed from an icon, the window menu will show the Open label because you can only open it from that state.

If you select Close from the window menu, the window and its associated pop-up windows are closed (converted to one icon), and no other commands are executed. If you select Open while on an icon, all associated pop-up windows are opened in the same state and position.

■ Full Size/Restore Size

The Full Size/Restore Size command item label toggles in the same way as Open/Close. If a window can be made bigger, the label reads Full Size, so that you can select it to make it full size (as determined by the application) and bring it to the front of the screen.

Once the window is its maximum size, the label changes to Restore Size. You select this to return it to the previous size.

■ Back

Select the Back command item to move a window or icon to the back of the workspace, behind other windows or icons.

■ Refresh

The Refresh command item redraws windows or icons.

■ Move

The Move command allows you to move the window to another area of the screen.

■ Resize

The Resize command lets you increase or decrease the size of the window.

■ Quit

Quit exits the window or icon.

Pop-Up Window Menu

A pop-up window menu is a menu you access from the header of a pop-up window (any window other than the base window). Figure 3-22 shows a pop-up window menu.

Figure 3-22: Pop-Up Window Menu

A pop-up window menu contains the following elements in addition to standard menu elements:

- Title: Window

- Dismiss

  Dismiss is a menu item with the following two choices:

  □ This Popup

    Dismiss the current pop-up window by selecting this command item.

  □ All Popups

    Select this item to dismiss all the pop-ups opened from the same base window.

- Back

  Back moves the window or icon to the back of the workspace, behind other windows or icons.

■ Refresh

Refresh redraws the pop-up window.

■ Owner?

The Owner? command item flashes the title bar of the base window that owns the pop-up window and brings the base window to the front of the screen. If the window is not owned by a base window (such as a pop-up window originating from the workspace menu), nothing happens.

■ Move

The Move command allows you to move the window to another area of the screen.

■ Resize

The Resize command allows you to increase or decrease the size of the window.

Settings Menus

Settings menus are found only in property windows. They put the button controls at the bottom of a property window in menu form.

The settings menu pops up whenever you press MENU within a property window. Figure 3-23 shows a settings menu. Notice that the items Apply, Reset, and Factory appear in the same order as the same buttons in the control area. They perform the same functions as well.

Figure 3-23: Settings Menu on the Miscellaneous Workspace Property Window

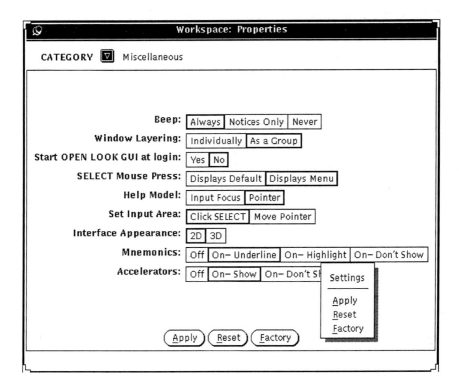

Scrollbar Menus

Scrollbar menus are used to reposition the data in the pane. The controls on the scrollbar menu are labeled according to whether they are accessed from a vertical scrollbar or a horizontal scrollbar. Figure 3-24 shows a scrollbar menu.

Figure 3-24: Vertical Scrollbar Menu

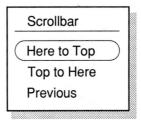

Vertical Scrollbar Menu

A vertical scrollbar menu contains the following elements:

- Title: Scrollbar

- Here to Top

  The Here to Top command item moves the object beside the pointer to the top of the pane.

- Top to Here

  The Top to Here command item moves the first object at the top of the pane to the pointer location.

- Previous

  The Previous command item returns the contents of the pane to the last scrolling position.

Horizontal Scrollbar Menu

A horizontal scrollbar menu contains the following elements:

- Title: Scrollbar

- Here to Left

  The Here to Left command item moves the object beside the pointer to the left of the pane.

- Left to Here

  The Left to Here command item moves the first object at the left of the pane to the pointer location.

- Previous

  Previous returns the contents of the pane to the last scrolling position.

Applications may provide more choices on the scrollbar menus.

4 THE OPEN LOOK Interface: Procedures

Introduction

Overview

This chapter contains procedures for operation of the features you read about in Chapter 3. If you want to perform the procedures in this chapter, you must use the mouse and its SELECT, ADJUST, and MENU buttons; you can also perform the procedures described in this chapter from the keyboard. Procedures for using the mouse and the keyboard, and performing basic tasks with each, are included in "Using the Mouse," "Using the Keyboard," and "Using the OPEN LOOK Interface" in Chapter 2.

Organization of the Chapter

The contents of this chapter are arranged as follows:

- Operating on Windows and Icons

  Supplies procedures for manipulating windows, panes, and icons.

- Operating on Menus

  Supplies procedures for viewing and choosing from menus and changing menu defaults.

- Scrollbars and Scrolling

  Explains how to manipulate scrollbars.

- Help Messages

  Explains how to get help text.

Operating on Windows and Icons

This section explains how to operate on windows, icons, and panes. Refer to the section, "Windows and Icons," in Chapter 3 if you need more information about any of the features.

Active Input Area

Only a window with active input focus can accept keyboard input. In order to type information from the keyboard into a text field or onto the pane of a window, you must designate one window as having active input focus. Set the active input area (the region or pane which accepts keyboard input) by clicking SELECT on the window pane or header; if you are using a keyboard, press 〔ALT〕 〔ESC〕 to establish active input focus in a window; press 〔ALT〕 〔F6〕 to move input focus to a window within an application.

A window with active input focus has a highlighted header and cursor. Once you establish the active input area in a window, you can move the pointer anywhere without losing input focus in that window. As you move input focus to different items within the window, they will become highlighted.

In a text field, you set the input focus by clicking SELECT or by pressing 〔TAB〕 to move to the text field in which you want to type. The insert point is the specific location of the active input area where characters are displayed. The insert point is marked by a caret to show the exact place where the characters you type on the keyboard are inserted into the text area.

If you attempt to establish active input focus in an area of the screen that does not accept keyboard input, the click is ignored and the input focus remains unchanged.

If you are using a keyboard to select active input focus, you will use the following keys in place of the mouse buttons.

- SELECT - 〔spacebar〕 or 〔CTRL〕 〔spacebar〕
- ADJUST - 〔CTRL〕 〔&〕
- MENU - 〔ALT〕 〔m〕 or 〔F4〕

NOTE | The keyboard equivalents shown above are the system default keystrokes. Although you may can change these defaults, these are the keystrokes used in this guide.

See Chapter 5, "The Workspace Manager Application," for information on how to change the current settings of keyboard equivalent key bindings.

Using the Window Menu

Each base window has a window menu, which controls that window's activities. You use the window menu to perform operations such as closing and quitting the window. To invoke the window menu, position the pointer on the header of a window or anywhere on an icon and press or click MENU.

 NOTE | If you invoke a pop-up window (including a help window) from an application, and then access the pop-up window menu from which you select "Back" (for background), the pop-up window retreats as expected behind the base window. However, if you then select "Back" from the base window's window menu, the pop-up window does not return to the front of the base window, but stays behind it.

To solve this problem when the pop-up is behind the base window, click SELECT on the header or border of the base window.

Opening Icons and Closing Windows

To close a window means to reduce the window to a small graphic symbol called an icon. You open the icon to convert it back to a window.

To close a window, do the following:

MOUSE:

1. Press MENU while in the window header.

2. Drag to Close and release MENU.

— or —

3. Close a window with the shortcut method by clicking SELECT on the window menu button, providing that the default menu item has not been changed.

KEYBD:

1. Press [**ALT**] [**F5**] or [**c**] to close the window.

To open an icon:

MOUSE:

1. Double-click SELECT on the icon, or position the pointer on the icon and press MENU.

2. Drag the pointer to Open and release MENU.

KEYBD:

1. Press [**SHIFT**] [**ESC**].

   A list of window options appears.

2. Press [**ALT**] [**F5**] or [**o**] to open the icon.

Note that if you close a base window that has an associated pop-up window, the pop-up window will also be closed.

Dismissing a Window

To dismiss from a base window:

MOUSE:

1. Access the window menu by pressing MENU while in the window header.

2. Drag the pointer to Quit and release MENU.

KEYBD:

1. Press [**ALT**] [**F4**] or [**q**].

To dismiss from a pop-up window:

MOUSE:

1. Access the window menu by pressing MENU while in the window header.

2. Drag the pointer to Dismiss and release MENU.

— or —

Click SELECT twice on the pushpin.

KEYBD:

1. Press (**SHIFT**) (**ESC**) to display a list of window options.

2. Press (→) to display the submenu for Dismiss.

The system displays two options:

– To close the current pop-up window, press (**ALT**) (**F9**) or type (**t**)

– To close ALL pop-up windows, press (**SHIFT**) (**ALT**) (**F9**) or press (**a**).

Moving Windows and Icons

To move a window or icon:

MOUSE:

1. Position the pointer on the header or border of the window, or anywhere on an icon.

2. Press SELECT and drag the object to its new location.

3. Release SELECT when the object reaches the desired location.

To move a window to the front of the screen:

1. Position the pointer anywhere in the window header except on the window menu button.

   2. Click SELECT.

KEYBD:

   1. Press `SHIFT` `ESC`.

   2. Press `ALT` `F7` or `m` to begin the Move procedure.

       A pointer appears within the object you are going to move.

   3. Use the `↓`, `↑`, `←`, and `→` keys to drag the window to the desired location.

   4. Press `F2` or `↵` to drop the object at the desired location.

If you want to cancel the drag operation once you begin moving an object, press `CTRL` `s`.

Resizing a Window

If a window has resize corners, you can shrink or expand it. If the new window size is too small to display a title or footer information, the information is either removed or truncated and an arrow (called a More arrow to indicate that more information exists) is displayed. The window cannot shrink below a minimum window size, which is determined by the application. Resizing does not change input focus.

Perform the following steps to resize a window:

MOUSE:

   1. Move the pointer to one of the resize corners of a window.

   2. Press SELECT and drag the pointer to a new location for the corner.

   3. Release SELECT. The window is repainted in its new size.

KEYBD:

   1. Press `SHIFT` `ESC`.

   2. Press `ALT` `F8` or `s` to begin the Resize procedure.

       A bent arrow appears within the object you are trying to move.

3. Use the ⬇, ⬆, ⬅, and ➡ keys to resize the window to the desired location.

4. Press ⟨**F2**⟩ to implement the newly sized window.

Dragging from one corner toward the opposite corner of the window reduces the window's size. Dragging away from the opposite corner enlarges the window's size. There is no change in the relative sizes of controls or graphics displayed in the window.

 NOTE If you make a Terminal Emulator window smaller, text is not redrawn for the smaller size and some of the text is obscured (does not wrap). Even if you enlarge the window, the obscured text does not return although subsequently entered text will properly wrap.

Accelerating with Double-Click

The double-click SELECT method is a shortcut way to perform operations without displaying a menu. You can:

Double-click SELECT in a header, but not on the window menu button, to display a window full size, or restore it to its previous size,

— or —

Double-click SELECT on an icon to open it.

Using Controls in Windows

A control area is a region of a window where application controls such as buttons and settings are displayed. A control area can be located anywhere in a base window, pop-up window, or in a pane within a base or pop-up window. Controls can be used to control more than one pane. Figure 4-1 shows controls at the top, right, and bottom of a window.

Figure 4-1: Control Areas

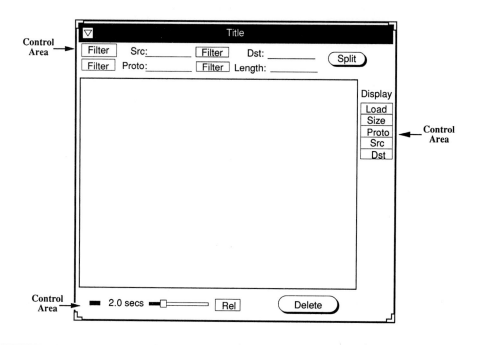

Using Buttons

Command buttons, which are labeled buttons with no window or menu mark, execute a single command with the following procedure:

MOUSE:

1. Move the pointer to the button.

2. Click SELECT.

   The button becomes highlighted (2D mode), or has a "depressed" appearance (3D mode) to indicate that it has been selected, and displays the standard busy pattern until it executes the command.

KEYBD:

1. Press (TAB) and (SHIFT) (TAB) to move to a button.

   The button becomes highlighted (2D mode), or has a "depressed" appearance (3D mode) to indicate that it has been selected.

2. Press (↵), the default action key, to execute the function.
   — or —
   From anywhere in the window, press (ALT) and the appropriate mnemonic.

Using Menu Buttons in a Control Area

A menu button is a button in a control area that has a triangular glyph to indicate an attached submenu.

MOUSE:

1. Invoke the submenu by moving the pointer to the menu button.

2. Press or click MENU to call up the menu in pop-up or stay-up mode.

KEYBD:

1. Press (TAB) and (SHIFT) (TAB) to move to a button.

   The button becomes highlighted (2D mode) or has a "depressed" appearance (3D mode) to indicate that it has been selected.

2. Press the (↓) key to display the submenu.

3. To exit the submenu, press (←).

If you want to execute the menu's default without accessing the submenu, you can change the "Select Mouse Press" setting on the miscellaneous workspace property window. Set it to "Displays Default" to execute the default from the menu button without invoking the submenu. "Displays Default" automatically executes the default when SELECT is clicked on a menu button or menu item. This gives you a quick and convenient way to perform a function you use frequently. See the subsection "Miscellaneous Workspace Property Window" in Chapter 5 and "Changing Menu Defaults" on page 17 for more information.

Using Sliders

Change the value of the slider setting with the following:

MOUSE:

1. Move the pointer to the slider drag box.

   Press SELECT and drag. The pointer stays in the drag box until the button is released.

2. Click SELECT to the left or right of the slider drag box on the bar to move the drag box one increment (default), or whatever the user-defined value is.

3. Click SELECT on end boxes.

KEYBD:

1. Move the input focus to the slider drag box.

2. Use the $\rightarrow$ and $\leftarrow$ keys to move the slider drag box to the left or right; use the $\uparrow$ and $\downarrow$ keys to move a vertical slider.

Using Text Fields

To type into a text field, follow these guidelines:

- Position the pointer on the text field exactly where you intend to type. This can be at the beginning of a blank line, or, if you want only to edit or add information, anywhere on a line that already has data in it.

- Click SELECT on the text field to give it active input focus. If you are using a keyboard, move the input focus on the text field by pressing (**TAB**). The caret, a small diamond that sits on the line of the text field, indicates the spot at which you can type. When you click SELECT on the part of the text field at which you want to type, the caret jumps to that spot.

- Press (**BACKSPACE**) to delete. If you want to delete characters from text that is already in place, move the pointer to the first character you want to delete and click SELECT to place the caret on that spot. Press (**BACKSPACE**) to delete characters behind the caret.

■ The amount of text you can type is not determined by the length of the text field line. When the field contains more text than it can show, the field scrolls to accommodate the text. See the subsection, "Text Fields" in the section "Controls" in Chapter 3 for more information on scrollable text fields.

■ To change text, you can "sweep" by pressing SELECT and dragging across the text to be deleted. The text will highlight. Type in the new data, and the highlighting will disappear. You cannot perform the "sweep" action if you are using a keyboard.

■ To delete the entire line of text, place the caret at the beginning of the line and press (**ALT**) (**SHIFT**) (**DELETE**).

■ To move easily from one field into another, you can use the "Next Field" and "Previous Field" keyboard keys instead of using the mouse to move the cursor. The default keys are (**TAB**) for Next Field, and (**SHIFT**) (**TAB**) for Previous Field. Each field acquires active input focus as you reach it.

You can use the following keys and modifiers in text fields:

Figure 4-2: Using the Keyboard in Text Fields

Key Combination	Editing Action
RIGHT	Move the caret forward one character
LEFT	Move the caret back one character
CTRL-RIGHT	Move the caret forward one word
CTRL-LEFT	Move the caret back one word
HOME	Move the caret to the beginning of the current line
END	Move the caret to the end of the current line
DELETE	Delete the character to the right of the caret
BACKSPACE	Delete the character to the left of the caret
CTRL-SHIFT-DELETE	Delete the word to the right of the caret
CTRL-SHIFT-BACKSPACE	Delete the word to the left of the caret
CTRL-DELETE	Delete to the end of the current line from the caret
CTRL-BACKSPACE	Delete to the beginning of the current line from the caret

The keystrokes listed above are the default keystrokes referred to in this guide; you may change these keystrokes if you wish.

Typing Text into a Command Window

When a command window is dismissed, it is removed from the screen. Any new information typed into that window before dismissing it is saved, whether or not a command has been executed. For example, if you are using a command window to copy a file, and you type newname into the text field, newname will remain in that text field until you execute the command or type new information into the text field. If you dismiss the window without executing the command, the word newname will still be in the copy window the next time you access it.

Using Property Windows

Property windows are pop-up windows that are used to change any or all of the characteristics of an application. Not all applications provide property windows. To use a property window from an application that has one, you do the following:

MOUSE:

1. Display a property window by selecting `Properties` from the menu.

   This will be the workspace menu or an application-supplied menu that provides a Properties selection.

2. Change settings in the property window. The application determines how you make changes: whether you type data into a text field, click SELECT, or choose from a menu.

3. When finished, click SELECT on the Apply button to finalize your changes and exit.

   — or —

   Click SELECT on the Reset button to undo your changes and return the properties to the previous settings, then click on Apply.

   — or —

   Select Reset to Factory to return the settings to the system-supplied defaults. Then select Apply to set those factory defaults.

KEYBD:

1. Type ⓞ to access the `Properties` menu. Change settings in the property window. The application determines how you make changes: whether you type data into a text field or choose from a menu.

2. When you finish making changes, press ⦅TAB⦆ to move the input focus to the `Apply` button.

   The button is selected.

3. Press ⦅spacebar⦆ to finalize your changes and exit.

Operating on Menus

This section explains how to operate on all of the OPEN LOOK Interface menus. Refer to the section "Menus" in Chapter 3 if you need definitions of any of the features mentioned in this section.

Pop-up and Stay-up Modes

There are two ways you can use the mouse in order to view and choose from any menu:

- Press-Drag-Release
- Click-Move-Click

As a result of these two methods, menus are displayed in two modes: pop-up and stay-up. You can also use the keyboard to navigate around menus. A pop-up menu appears by using the press-drag-release method of viewing and choosing from menus. A stay-up menu appears by using the click-move-click method of viewing and choosing from menus.

Choosing from a Menu with Press-Drag-Release

Press-drag-release displays a pop-up menu, which stays on the screen only as long as you press the MENU button.

1. Press and hold down MENU while moving the pointer from item to item.

   The pop-up menu that corresponds to the pointer location appears.

   In 2D mode, when the pointer is on an item, the item acquires the button-shaped outline and is highlighted by becoming dark with white type. In 3D mode, a depressed, button-shaped outline appears. When the pointer is off the item, it returns to its normal condition.

2. Once the pointer is on the item you want, release MENU. The action is initiated, and the menu is dismissed. If you release MENU after you move the pointer off the menu, the menu is dismissed and no action is initiated.

Choosing from a Menu with Click-Move-Click

Click-move-click displays a stay-up menu, which stays on the screen until you move the pointer off the menu and click SELECT or MENU somewhere else. You do not have to keep the MENU button pressed as you do with the press-drag-release method. Perform the following procedure:

1. Click MENU . The menu that corresponds to the pointer location appears and stays up.

2. Move the pointer to the control you want to choose. There is no visual feedback as you move the pointer.

3. Perform one of the following:

   Click SELECT on a command item to execute the command,

   — or —

   Click MENU on a menu item to display a submenu in stay-up mode, then click SELECT on an item on the submenu.

   — or —

   If you have set up the submenu with a default menu item, click SELECT on a menu item to execute the submenu default.

   — or —

   Press ⏎ to activate the default item.

   — or —

   Use the TAB key to move focus to the desired item and press spacebar .

Choosing from a Menu with Combined Operations

You can combine select-move-select and press-drag-release operations. If a menu is displayed in stay-up mode by clicking MENU, you can then move the pointer into a submenu and view it by pressing MENU.

Using the Keyboard to Move Around Menus

Keyboard navigation. Allows you to select the active input area using the [TAB], and [SHIFT] [TAB] navigation keys on the keyboard.

- The [SHIFT] [TAB] key moves the input focus to the previous menu item. If the input focus is on the first item of the menu, pressing [SHIFT] [TAB] will wrap to the last item of the menu.

- The [TAB] key moves the input focus to the next menu item. If the input focus is on the last item of the menu, then pressing [TAB] will wrap to the first item of the menu.

- The [CANCEL] or [ESC] key will unpost the menu and leave the input focus on the menu button.

- If input focus is on a menu button within a menu, pressing [CTRL] [m] or [F4] will post the submenu associated with the menu button or pressing an arrow key ([→] or [↓]) that is in the same direction as the menu button's menu mark.

Using a Pushpin on a Menu

A pushpin allows a menu to stay "pinned" to the screen for as long as you want to keep it. When you pin a menu, it disappears briefly and returns as a pop-up command window with all the attributes and functionality of a command window: the title, pushpin, and pop-up window menu. The menu items, however, while performing all the functions of buttons, do not acquire the shape of buttons. A pinned menu stays on the screen even if you select a command and execute it.

To pin a menu,

MOUSE:

1. Move the pointer to the pushpin.

2. Click SELECT.

    The pin pops into the hole.

3. To dismiss a pinned meu, click SELECT on the pushpin. This does not convert it from a command window back into a menu; it dismisses it.

KEYBD:

1. Press $\boxed{\text{CTRL}}$ $\boxed{\text{t}}$.

    This pins the menu when the pushpin is out, or dismisses a pinned menu when the pushpin is in.

Changing Menu Defaults

Although the OPEN LOOK Interface supplies menu default choices, you may wish to change the default settings to settings that suit your work needs. You can change the menu default at any time by using the default modifier key. The modifier key supplied by the OPEN LOOK Interface is $\boxed{\text{CTRL}}$. (This modifier key can be changed with the Mouse Settings workspace property window described in in Chapter 5.)

Perform the following procedure to change a menu default with the modifier key:

MOUSE:

1. Press MENU with the pointer on a menu button in a control area. The menu is displayed. The default outline appears around the default setting.

2. Move the pointer to the current default.

3. Continue pressing MENU and press $\boxed{\text{CTRL}}$ (or whatever you have designated as the modifier key) on the keyboard.

4. Drag the pointer to the item you want as the new default. The default outline follows from button to button until you make a selection.

5. Release MENU to set the default and remove the menu from the screen.

6. Release ⟨**CTRL**⟩.

| NOTE | The system requires evidence of mouse motion for this procedure to work. If you get no response while pressing the modifier key while changing the default, try jiggling the mouse a bit as you press the modifier. |

KEYBD:

1. Press ⟨**TAB**⟩ to select a menu button in a control area.

2. Press ⟨**SHIFT**⟩ while holding down the ⟨**CTRL**⟩ ⟨**m**⟩ or ⟨**F4**⟩ keys.

Scrollbars and Scrolling

Scrollbars appear next to a pane when the pane contains scrollable information. They enable you to change the view of the data that is displayed in a pane, or move directly to the beginning or end of the information available in a pane.

Vertical scrollbars are located at the right of the pane. Horizontal scrollbars are positioned at the bottom of a pane. A pane can have both vertical and horizontal scrollbars, which work in exactly the same way.

The components of a scrollbar are:

- Cable
- Elevator
- Cable anchors

The components are the same in both vertical and horizontal scrollbars, but the up and down arrows in the vertical scrollbar become left and right arrows in the horizontal scrollbar, and the top and bottom cable anchors are called left and right cable anchors.

Figure 4-3 and Figure 4-4 show horizontal and vertical scrollbars.

Figure 4-3: A Horizontal Scrollbar

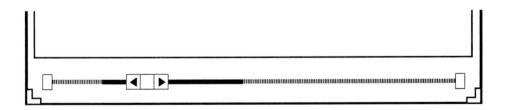

Figure 4-4: Vertical Scrollbar Components

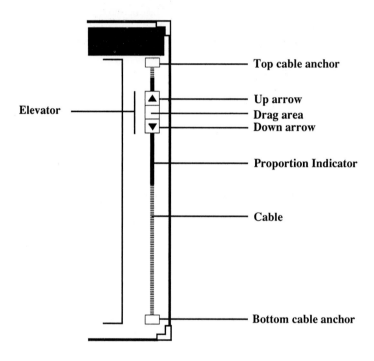

Abbreviated Scrollbar

A complete scrollbar is displayed whenever possible. When the pane is too small to show a scrollbar and cable, however, the cable is not displayed. When a pane is too small to show the top and bottom cable anchors and the elevator, an abbreviated scrollbar is displayed. The abbreviated scrollbar has cable anchors and up and down arrows, but no drag area. It is also possible to display a minimum scrollbar which is the minumum size of the pane; this scrollbar consists of only the up and down arrows.

Note that the minimum size of a pane with a scrollbar is the size of the abbreviated scrollbar. A pane with a scrollbar cannot be made smaller than the dimensions of the abbreviated scrollbar.

Scrollbar Cable

The length of the scrollbar cable represents the total size of the data from the application that can be viewed in increments. The scrollbar cable proportion indicator, attached to the elevator, is the dark area of the cable that shows the portion of the total text visible in the pane.

Figure 4-5: Scrollbar Positioning

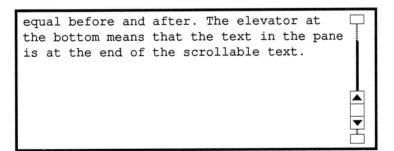

Elevator

The location of the elevator shows the position of the pane in the total data represented by the cable, as shown in Figure 4-5. The elevator in the middle means that the amount of scrollable text is equal before and after. The elevator at the bottom means that the text in the pane is at the end of the scrollable text.

Scrollbar Operation

Use the SELECT mouse button to manipulate the scrollbar, as described in the following subsections.

Move forward or backward

Move the pointer into the drag area and press SELECT. Drag the pointer in the drag area of the elevator to move the view in the pane forward or backward. The drag area becomes highlighted, and the pointer rides the drag area. The contents of the pane are updated as you drag the elevator.

Release SELECT. The drag area ceases to be highlighted.

You can move to a relative position in a large file, without having to wait for all the data to scroll through the pane. The scrolling display can jump ahead to the new point in the data.

Move up and down one unit

MOUSE:

> When you click SELECT on the up arrow, it is highlighted until the elevator moves up one unit to display one new unit at the top of the pane. If you click SELECT on the down arrow, the down arrow is highlighted until the elevator moves down one unit to display one new unit at the bottom of the pane.

KEYBD:

> Press (TAB) to establish active input focus on the pane. Use (PAGEUP) and (PAGEDOWN) to move up and down one unit.
>
> Use (ALT) (↓) or (ALT) (↑) to move one unit to the left or right.

Move up and down one pane

MOUSE:

Click SELECT below the elevator anywhere in the scrollbar region between the elevator and the bottom cable anchor to move the view on the data up one pane. Click SELECT above the elevator to move the view down one pane. Press SELECT to repeat the action. The pointer will, if necessary, jump ahead on the cable to stay out of the way of the elevator.

KEYBD:

Press (**TAB**) to establish active input focus on the pane; it will highlight. Use (**CTRL**) (**PAGEUP**) and (**CTRL**) (**PAGEDOWN**) to move up and down one pane.

Use (**CTRL**) (**{**) or (**CTRL**) (**}**) to move one pane left or right.

Move to the beginning or end

MOUSE:

Click SELECT on the top cable anchor to move the view to the beginning of the data. The top cable anchor will highlight, and the view will move to show the beginning of the data. The elevator will move to the top of the pane, with the proportion indicator displayed below it, and the top cable anchor will then return to its normal state.

To move the view to the end of the data, click SELECT on the bottom cable anchor. The bottom cable anchor will highlight, and the view will move to show the end of the data. The last line of the contents will be displayed in the middle of the pane. The elevator will move to the bottom of the pane, with the proportion indicator displayed above it, and the bottom cable anchor will then return to its normal state.

KEYBD:

Use (**ALT**) (**PAGEUP**) to scroll to the beginning of the data. Use (**ALT**) (**PAGEDOWN**) to scroll to the end of the data.

Use (**ALT**) (**SHIFT**) (**{**) to scroll to the left edge of the pane. Use (**ALT**) (**SHIFT**) (**}**) to scroll to the right edge of the pane.

NOTE If you are using a mouse to drag on a vertical scrollbar, paging indicators will appear if there are several pages of information to view. These page number indicators appear to the right of the scrollbar and change as you scroll to a new page. Paging indicators DO NOT appear if you are using a keyboard.

Using Scrollbar Menus

You use the scrollbar menu to move text within the pane. This menu is used when there is hidden text to be scrolled.

Moving Here to Top

To move a line of text from the middle of the pane to the top of the pane:

MOUSE:

1. Move the pointer so that it is in the scrollbar area next to the line of text.

2. Press MENU to display the Scrollbar menu at the pointer location.

3. Drag to the re to Toptem.

4. Release MENU. The Scrollbar menu is dismissed, and the view in the pane has changed so that the line next to the pointer is at the top of the pane. The pointer's position does not change.

Moving Top to Here

To move a line of text from the top of the pane, follow the procedures described in the previous section, "Moving Here to Top," but select the Top to Here item.

Help Messages

The OPEN LOOK Interface has on-line help messages that give you information about the interface and its various elements, and about applications. Help is available for most OPEN LOOK objects. If not, the message, `There is no help available for this object`, is displayed.

Not every keyboard has a key labeled "HELP." The f1 function key is the default key provided by the OPEN LOOK Interface for help. You can change the default for the help key from the keyboard settings workspace property window. (See Chapter 5 for information on the workspace property windows.)

The help window has all the standard elements of a pop-up window, with a pane, but no control area. A help window has a magnifying glass, which displays the object for which you are requesting help, to the left of the text.

The help window is pinned when it arrives on the screen. You keep the help window up as long as you need it, and dismiss it by clicking SELECT on the pushpin to unpin it.

If you are using a keyboard, use ⌧TAB⌧ to move input focus on the item for which you are requesting help. Then press ⌧F1⌧. See Figure 4-6 for a sample help window.

NOTE   When using a curses application (such as FACE) within a Terminal Emulator window, the OPEN LOOK Interface intercepts ⌧F1⌧ (or any function key designated for help) and interprets it as a request for help. This creates a conflict with applications that use ⌧F1⌧ or other function keys to perform their own specific functions.

To avoid this situation, use the keyboard settings workspace property window to reset the help key to a key not used by the application.

Figure 4-6: Help Window

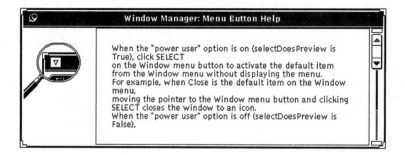

Accessing Help

You access a help window with the following procedure:

MOUSE:

1. Move the pointer to the object with which you need help.

2. Press the help key on the keyboard. A pinned help window is displayed.

3. Dismiss the help window by clicking SELECT on the pushpin to unpin it, or by pressing MENU on the window header and selecting Dismiss from the menu.

KEYBD:

1. Move input focus to the object with which you need help. Use the [**TAB**] or [**SHIFT**] [**TAB**] keys to do this.

2. Press [**F1**], the help key.

   A pinned window is displayed.

3. To dismiss the window, press [**CTRL**] [**t**] or press [**CTRL**] [**m**] to access the menu; then select Dismiss.

> **NOTE** You can get help from the keyboard ONLY if the Help Model option is set to Input Focus on the Miscellaneous Workspace property sheet. If this option is set to Pointer, you can only access the Help function using a mouse. See Chapter 5 for more information on the Miscellanous Workspace property sheet settings.

Move the pointer to another object in the same application and press the help key again. Help information for the other object replaces the display in the pane of the first help window.

If one help window is displayed and you move the pointer to another application and press the help key, another help window is displayed with help for the second application.

5 The Workspace Manager Application

Introduction

The Workspace Manager application helps the OPEN LOOK Graphical User Interface manage applications, execute programs, and customize your OPEN LOOK interface environment. The Workspace menu gives you access to these applications and programs, with menu item selections for Terminal Emulator, Pixmap Editor, File Manager, Administration Manager, and Print Screen applications, as well as any other programs your site has installed. The Workspace menu also has an Exit item which allows you to exit the entire OPEN LOOK Interface environment.

The Properties menu item on the Workspace menu gives you a submenu of Workspace Property windows. The Workspace property windows are important because you use them to change settings globally for all of the OPEN LOOK Interface.

Organization of the Chapter

This chapter is devoted to the Workspace property windows and how to use them. Subsections include information on the following:

- Programs Submenu workspace property window
- Icons workspace property window
- Color workspace property window
- Mouse Settings workspace property window
- Mouse Modifiers workspace property window
- Keyboard Functions workspace property windows
- Miscellaneous workspace property window

The Workspace Property Windows

The Workspace property windows available from the Properties menu item on the Workspace menu enable you to customize settings for the following OPEN LOOK Interface functions:

- Programs Submenu

  Supplies the list of programs available from the Programs menu item on the Workspace menu.

- Icons

  Defines placement and appearance of icons.

- Color

  Sets color properties of the OPEN LOOK Interface.

- Mouse Modifiers

  Defines the mouse buttons and functions.

- Mouse Settings

  Defines mouse click and mouse movement.

- Keyboard Functions

  Sets application-supported keyboard equivalent functions.

- Miscellaneous

  Defines settings for the system beep, window layering function, automatic startup, help model, input focus model, interface appearance, display of mnemonics and accelerators, and the use of the SELECT mouse button on a menu button.

Workspace Property Window Elements

Each Workspace property window has the following elements:

- Title: Properties
- Pushpin

- CATEGORY button

  Select this button to move between the different property sheets within a property window, without having to return to the Properties submenu. When you make changes in one property window and switch to another property window without applying those changes, a change bar appears next to the CATEGORY button.

- Changes bars

  Vertical bars that appear next to an item you edit on a property sheet, indicating that a change has been made. These change bars remain next to an item until you select Apply and implement the changes.

- Apply button

  Select this button to validate the current values on the screen and save the changes made. If you make changes to one property sheet and switch to another sheet without applying those changes, the Apply button becomes Apply All, and the Dismiss button becomes Cancel. You can make many changes on different property sheets and then apply all the changes or cancel all the changes at once.

- Reset button

  Select this button to return the property settings to their currently saved values.

- Reset to Factory button.

  Select this button to reset the property settings to the defaults originally provided with the system.

The Apply, Reset, and Reset to Factory buttons, displayed at the bottom of the Property sheet windows, can be accessed by using the appropriate mnemonics, shown below:

- Apply. `ALT` `a`
- Reset. `ALT` `r`
- Reset to Factory. `ALT` `f`

You can also press `spacebar` while a button is selected in order to activate the button.

Programs Submenu Workspace Property Window

The Programs Submenu workspace property window lets you add, delete, or change program names listed in the programs submenu of the Workspace menu (accessed by selecting Programs from the Workspace menu).

Figure 5-1 shows the Programs Submenu workspace property window.

Figure 5-1: Programs Submenu Workspace Property Window

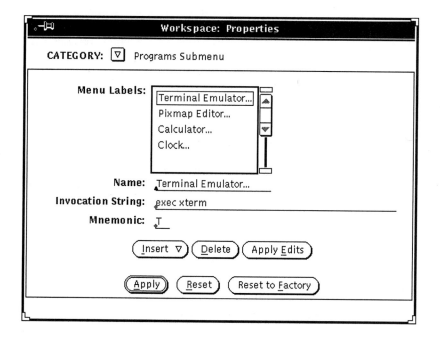

OPEN LOOK GUI User's Guide: Release 4

The Programs Submenu workspace property window contains the following elements in addition to the required elements:

- An editable scrolling list labeled "Menu Labels."

  The scrolling list can be "scrolled," or paged through, to view information that is too extensive to fit into one window or portion of a window. This scrolling list defines the programs accessible from the Programs menu item of the Workspace menu.

  You edit the scrolling list by choosing an item to identify as the current item.

- A text field labeled "Name."

  The information you type in this field becomes the label on the Programs submenu item for that program.

- A text field labeled "Invocation String".

  The information you type in this field is the string used to execute the named program.

- A text field labeled "Mnemonic".

  The information you type in this field is the character you want to use as the mnemonic for the menu item. All mnemonics should be one character in length and must be unique.

- Insert menu button.

  This menu button has a submenu with the following two buttons:

  - Before. This is used to insert information before the currently chosen item.

  - After. This is used to insert information after the currently chosen item.

- Delete button.

  This button is used to delete the currently chosen item from the scrolling list.

■ Apply Edits button

Select this button to finalize your changes to the currently chosen item.

Adding a New Menu Item

To access the Programs submenu property window, click SELECT on the Programs Submenu menu item or type the mnemonic ⌐p.⌐

To add a new menu item to the Programs submenu of the Workspace menu:

MOUSE:

1. Decide where on the list you want to add the new menu item. Click SELECT on an item in the editable scrolling list. The chosen item highlights and acquires a rectangular border.

2. Press MENU on the Insert button, to insert the new item before or after the chosen item.

3. A submenu with the selections Before and After appears.

   – If you want the new name inserted before the chosen item, drag the pointer to Before and release.

   – If you want the new name inserted after the chosen item, drag the pointer to After and release.

   The outline around the chosen item moves to a position above or below the selected item. This is where the new name will appear.

   Input focus automatically moves to the Name text field. Type the new name and press ⌐↵⌐.

   Input focus moves to the Invocation String text field.

4. Type the invocation string for the program and press ⌐↵⌐.

   Input focus moves to the Mnemonic text field.

5. Type the character you want to use as the mnemonic for the menu item and press ⌐↵⌐.

6. Input focus moves to the Apply Edits button and the new name appears in the scrolling list.

7. Click SELECT on Apply Edits to save your changes.

NOTE You must select Apply Edits for each item you change, but you can save changes to more than one item using Apply. A vertical change bar appears to the left of each text field that you change. When you select Apply Edits, the change bar disappears and a change bar appears next to Menu Labels. When Apply is selected, the change bar next to Menu Labels disappears.

KEYBD:

1. Decide where on the list you want to add the new menu item. Use **TAB** or **SHIFT** **TAB** to move input focus to the scrolling list. Use the ⬆ and ⬇ keys to move to items within the scrolling list.

2. Press **spacebar**.

3. Press **ALT** **i** to select the Insert button and display its submenu. The choices Before and After appear on the submenu.

4. If you want to add the new menu item after the chosen item on the scrolling list, make sure the highlighting is on After; if it is not, press ⬇ to position the highlighting on After. If you want to add the item before the chosen item on the scrolling list, make sure the highlighting is on Before; if it is not, press ⬆ to move the highlighting.

5. Press **spacebar**.

   The outline around the chosen item moves to a position above or below the selected item; this is where the new name will appear.

   The input focus automatically moves to the Name text field. The small pointer at the beginning of the field will blink.

6. Type the new item name.

7. Press **TAB** or ⏎ to move to the next field, Invocation String.

8. Type the invocation string for the program.

9. Press **TAB** or ⏎ to move to the next field, Mnemonic.

10. If desired, enter a mnemonic name and press ⏎ to transfer input focus to Apply Edits.

11. Press ⟨ **spacebar** ⟩ to apply the changes you made.

12. Press ⟨ **TAB** ⟩ until the Apply button is selected or just press ⏎.

13. Press ⟨ **spacebar** ⟩ to save the changes and dismiss the property window.

Editing or Changing an Item

To edit an existing item name or change the invocation string:

MOUSE:

1. Click SELECT on the item in the scrolling list that you wish to change. The name of that item will be displayed in the Name field and its invocation string in the Invocation String field. If the item has a mnemonic associated with it, it will be displayed in the Mnemonic text field.

2. Edit the existing information by clicking SELECT on the text field to give it active input focus. The small triangle, the caret, jumps to the space you have selected. You type to insert text here. Use the ⟨ **BACKSPACE** ⟩ key to delete characters behind the caret.

3. Click SELECT on the Apply Edits button when finished.

4. Click SELECT on the Apply button to save your changes to the list and dismiss the property window.

KEYBD:

1. Use ⟨ **TAB** ⟩ or ⟨ **SHIFT** ⟩ ⟨ **TAB** ⟩ and the ⟨↑⟩ and ⟨↓⟩ keys to move input focus to the item on the scrolling list that you want to edit.

2. Press ⟨ **spacebar** ⟩ to select the item.

   The name of the item will be displayed in the Name field and its invocation string will appear in the Invocation String field. If the item has a mnemonics associated with it, it will be displayed in the Mnemonic text field.

3. Press [TAB] to move to the desired text field.

   The caret is positioned at the beginning of the text field and will blink to indicate that it is ready for you to insert text.

4. Type the desired text; use the [BACKSPACE] key to delete characters behind the caret.

5. Press [ALT] [e] to select the Apply Edits button.

6. Press [↵] to select the Apply button.

Deleting an Item from the Scrolling List

To delete an item, do the following:

MOUSE:

1. Click SELECT on the name of the item you want removed from the list.

2. Click SELECT on the Delete button.

3. Click SELECT on Apply to save your changes and dismiss the property window.

KEYBD:

1. Use [TAB] or [SHIFT] [TAB] and the [↑] or [↓] keys to move input focus to the item on the list that you want to delete.

2. Press [spacebar].

3. Press [ALT] [d] to select the Delete button.

4. Press [↵] to select the Apply button.

 NOTE If more than one change is to be made in the programs submenu, pin the property window before you select the Apply button. Don't unpin the property window until all changes are made and applied.

Icons Workspace Property Window

The icons property window defines placement and appearance of icons. There are two icons property settings:

- Location. The Location setting determines the side of the screen where icons are placed. The values are Top, Bottom (which is the factory setting), Left, and Right.

- Border. The Border setting determines whether icon borders are displayed or suppressed in color implementations. Values are Show or Don't Show; the default is Show. The border is always shown for monochrome displays.

The Icons property window can be accessed by selecting Icons from the Properties submenu or by using the mnemonic $\boxed{i}$.

Color Workspace Property Window

The Color workspace property window, shown in Figure 5-2, has a Color Combinations abbreviated menu button which allows you to select a palette of custom colors for your OPEN LOOK environment. When you select this button, a list of custom color combinations is displayed. When you choose a custom option, the different parts of the window will automatically be set to a particular color; you do not have to individually choose a color for each part of the window.

Beneath the Custom button is a row of color choices. Below the color choices, on the left-hand side of the window, are six elements. Each element has a box to the right of it; this box displays the color as you choose it from the Color Choices bar.

The Color Sample window to the right of the color boxes immediately reflects your selections as you make them. You can view as many color combinations as you wish until you select Apply.

You can change the colors for the following six elements:

- Workspace.

  This changes the color of the workspace.

- Window Background.

  This changes the color for the window background.

- Input Window.

  This determines the color of the window header that contains the active input area.

- Input Focus.

  This changes the color of the active caret which indicates where the current input focus is; this also determines the color that is displayed for input focus highlighting.

- Text Foreground.

  This changes the color of the text used in a text pane.

- Text Background.

  This changes the color of the background of a text pane.

To access the Color property window, click select on Color from the Properties submenu or type the mnemonic, c.

The Color workspace property window can be used for black and white (or single color) screens to invert the dark and light colors, and with grayscale screens to adjust shades of gray. If you have a color system, the Color workspace property window defines the color properties of the workspace.

Figure 5-2: Color Workspace Property Window

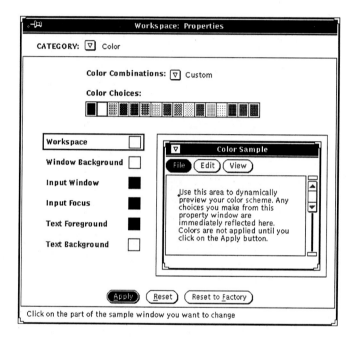

It is easy to view and select any number of color combinations with the steps provided below. With a mouse, you can change colors using the Color Sample on the right side of the window, or the list of elements on the left side of the window.

MOUSE:

1. Move the pointer over the part of the Color Sample window that you want to change; click SELECT.

   A border appears around the corresponding element to the left of the Color Sample.

   — or —

   Move the pointer to the list of elements and click SELECT on the desired element.

   A border appears around the element you selected.

2. Move the pointer to the Color Choices bar at the top of the window and click SELECT on the desired color.

   The box next to the selected element becomes filled with the color you chose, as does the feature itself in the sample window on the right side of the screen. A vertical change bar appears to the left of the selected element to indicate that you have changed it.

3. Change any or all of the settings as frequently as you wish. Make all the changes you want and when you are finished, click SELECT on Apply.

   This saves your changes and dismisses the property window.

KEYBD:

1. Press [ALT] [ESC] to establish input focus in the window, if necessary.

2. Press [SHIFT] [TAB] to move the highlighting to the list of elements. Use the [↑] and [↓] keys to move to the element you want to change.

3. Press [spacebar] to select the element.

   The element you selected becomes highlighted.

4. Press [SHIFT] [TAB] to move the highlighting to the Color Choices bar at the top of the window.

5. Use the [←] and [→] keys to move to different colors within the bar.

   A border appears around the current color.

6. Press (**spacebar**) to choose the desired color.

   The box next to the selected element becomes filled with the color you chose, as does the feature itself in the sample window on the right side of the screen. A vertical change bar appears to the left of the selected element to indicate that you have changed it.

7. When you finish making all changes, press (**TAB**) until the Apply button is selected; then press (**spacebar**) to save the changes you made and dismiss the property window.

The Color workspace properties window for monochrome displays consists of two exclusive settings: "Black on White" (the default), and "White on Black."

The colors for icons, window background and window foreground, and input focus color, for example, can also be set from some applications. If this is done, those settings override settings made from the Color workspace property window.

If you set the input window header color to be the same as the window background color, the Window Manager swaps the window background color with the window foreground color so that the window title will be visible.

 NOTE   You cannot set window foreground color (labels in buttons, and control captions, for example) from the Color workspace properties window. The default is black or white, depending on window background.

Mouse Modifiers Workspace Property Window

The Mouse Modifiers workspace property window defines which combination of keys and mouse buttons perform the SELECT, ADJUST, MENU, Constrain, Duplicate, Scroll by Panning, and Set Menu Default functions. To access the Mouse Modifiers property window, select the Mouse Modifiers option from the Properties submenu or use the mnemonic (**o**).

Figure 5-3: Mouse Modifiers Workspace Property Window

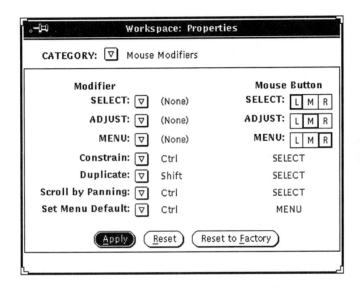

The Mouse Modifiers workspace property window has two columns, labeled Modifier and Mouse Button.

The Modifier column contains abbreviated menu buttons with labels of SELECT, ADJUST, MENU, Constrain, Duplicate, Scroll by Panning, and Set Menu Default.

The first three items in the property window — SELECT, ADJUST, and MENU — refer to the functions assigned to the mouse buttons. The column beside these items defines the modifier key used to enable a one- or two-button mouse to provide the three functions.

The available modifiers are shown below. You can use none, one, or a combination of one or more.

- None

- Shift

- CTRL

- Alt

The modifier shown in Figure 5-3 is "None." This means that there is no modifier supplementing the existing mouse buttons, because a three-button mouse has a dedicated button for each of the SELECT, ADJUST, and MENU functions. However, if you have a one- or two-button mouse, you must add the (**SHIFT**), (**CTRL**), or (**ALT**) key on your keyboard to work in conjunction with the mouse button or buttons in order to provide all three functions.

Constrain, Duplicate, and Scroll by Panning are used only if you are running applications that use these functions. The default for these functions are shown below.

- Constrain. CTRL

- Duplicate. Shift

- Scroll by panning. CTRL

- Set Menu Default. CTRL

Refer to the documentation that accompanies the application software to learn if your application supports these settings.

Set Menu Default enables you to change the default item on a menu. You use the modifier key with the mouse button to change the menu default.

The Mouse Button column contains three rows, of exclusive settings with values L, M, and R, for Left, Middle, and Right mouse buttons. If you are left-handed, you may wish to reverse the mouse buttons. Click SELECT on L, M, or R, to choose a new location for the specified functions.

To view the modifier submenu for the items listed on the Mouse Modifiers window follow these procedures:

MOUSE:

    Press MENU on an abbreviated menu button.

KEYBD:

    Press ⬚**TAB** to select an abbreviated menu button.

    Press ⬚**F4** to display the submenu.

Mouse Settings Workspace Property Window

This property sheet is used to set the various options available when using a mouse. You can change the options by adjusting the slider displayed in the window.

Figure 5-4: Mouse Settings Workspace Property Window

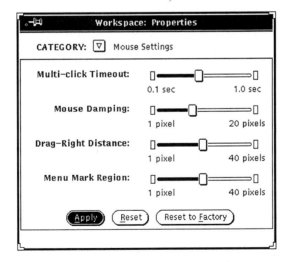

The mouse features you may change include:

- Multi-click Timeout

- Mouse Damping

- Drag-Right Distance

- Menu Mark Region

The multi-click timeout feature allows you to determine the maximum time between clicks of the mouse button. For example, if the time lapse between mouse clicks is longer than the multi-click timeout setting, the system treats the clicks as two separate commands, rather than a single command.

The mouse damping feature lets you determine how far the mouse must be moved before the system recognizes the movement.

The drag-right distance feature allows you to specify how far you must drag the pointer to the right in order to display a submenu.

The menu mark region is the opposite of drag-right. This feature lets you specify how far left to move the pointer off the menu in order to pop down a menu.

To change the settings using a mouse, position the pointer to the left or right of the slider and click SELECT until you reach the desired setting. If you are using a keyboard, press [ALT] [ESC] to establish input focus in the window (if necessary). Use the [TAB] and [↑] [↓] keys to move to a feature. Press [→] and [←] to move the slider to the desired setting. Select Apply to implement the changes.

Keyboard Functions Workspace Property Windows

The Keyboard Functions workspace property window, shown in Figure 5-5, enables you to view and modify the settings of the various types of keyboard equivalent bindings. The key bindings are grouped into the following functional categories, each with its own property sheet:

- Core Functions

- Mouse Functions

- Navigation

- Scrolling

- Text Selection keys

- Text Editing keys

- System Keys

 NOTE Take care when choosing keyboard equivalents which may have a conflicting meaning/function within the system. (CTRL) (ALT) (d), for example, should NOT be used as an accelerator on some systems, since it can cause unwanted behavior or may cause the system to halt.

Keyboard settings can be function keys, such as F1 through F12, or they can be a combination of modifier keys and function or other primary keys.

When you change the key bindings, the change is effective as soon as you select Apply.

Figure 5-5: Keyboard Functions Workspace Property Window

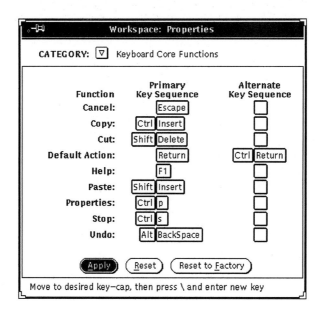

Typical modifier keys are (**SHIFT**), (**CTRL**), or (**ALT**); your keyboard may have others.

Some of the functions listed on the Keyboard Functions workspace property window are provided as part of the OPEN LOOK interface (called core functions), and others are application-dependent, meaning that they can work only if you are running applications that support those functions.

Core Functions Property Sheet

Core functions supported by OPEN LOOK are Cut, Copy, Paste, Help, Next Field, and Previous Field. Refer to the documentation that accompanies the application software to learn if your application supports functions such as Cancel, Properties, Stop, and Undo, and how it uses these functions. Defaults are shown in Figure 5-5.

The following functions can be defined with this workspace property window.

- Cancel.

    The default is (ESC) with no modifier.

- Copy.

    Copy enables you to make a copy of a selected object (such as a block of text) and put it into a clipboard, which is an area that keeps track of data that is cut or copied. Default is (CTRL) (INSERT).

- Cut.

    Cut makes a copy of the selected object and puts in into a clipboard, then deletes the object from the workspace. Default is (SHIFT) (DELETE).

- Help.

    Help displays a help window for the object under the pointer. Default is (F1).

- Paste.

    Paste inserts a copy of the clipboard data at the insert point. Default is (SHIFT) (INSERT).

- Properties.

    The default is (CTRL) (p).

- Stop.

    The default is (CTRL) (s).

- Undo.

    The default is (ALT) (BACKSPACE).

■ Default Action.

.

Be aware that if you are running applications not provided by the OPEN LOOK interface (such as a text editor in an xterm window), some of the keystrokes that fulfill functions in that application may already be in use by OPEN LOOK. The OPEN LOOK-defined key mapping will override a non-OPEN LOOK application's key mapping. For example, if you are using an application which defines (CTRL) (c) as quitting the application, then when you press that combination of keys, you will get the OPEN LOOK-defined default, which is copy. You can solve this conflict by mapping your OPEN LOOK functions to different keys. Compare the OPEN LOOK defaults with any keystroke functions used by the application in question, and change the key combinations on this property window so they are different.

Changing Keyboard Settings

Each keyboard property sheet contains two columns, "Primary" and "Alternate" key sequences. The alternate key sequence simply provides an additional binding for the key, which is used when an application has already used the primary key sequence for another function and there is a conflict with the primary key sequence. For example, the alternate key sequences for the Next Field and Prev Field keys are intended for use in text fields and panes where the primary key sequences are valid input characters.

| NOTE | New key bindings that you enter are validated for uniqueness against all existing key bindings, not only those on the same property sheet. If a duplicate key binding is detected, the system displays a notice box describing the function and its duplicate key binding. |

If you want to change a key sequence, do the following:

MOUSE:

1. Press SELECT on the imary Key Sequencer Alternate Key Sequence you want to edit.

   The key sequence becomes highlighted.

2. Press the ` (back quote) or the \ (backslash) key.

3. The next complete keystroke that you enter is understood to be the new key binding for the currently selected item.

   A complete keystroke consists of one or more modifiers (SHIFT, CTRL, or ALT, for example) plus another key.

4. If you change your mind, you can press (ALT) (BACKSPACE) to undo the key sequence. To delete an alternate key sequence, press (DELETE) or (BACKSPACE).

5. Click SELECT on Apply to save your changes and dismiss the property window.

KEYBD:

1. Press (TAB) or (SHIFT) (TAB) and the arrow keys to move input focus to the item you want to change.

2. Press the ` (back quote) or the \ (backslash) key.

3. The next complete keystroke that you enter is understood to be the new key binding for the currently selected item.

   A complete keystroke consists of a modifier (SHIFT, CTRL, ALT) plus another key.

   If you change your mind, you can press (ALT) (BACKSPACE) to undo the key sequence. To delete an alternate key sequence, press (DELETE) or (BACKSPACE).

4. Press (TAB) to select Apply; press (spacebar) to save your changes.

The Keyboard Properties Submenu

The Keyboard Properties submenu has the following options; the corresponding mnemonic for each option is shown.

- Core Functions. (c)
- Mouse Modifiers. (m)
- Navigation. (n)

- Scrolling. $\boxed{\text{s}}$
- Text Selection. $\boxed{\text{l}}$
- Text Editing. $\boxed{\text{e}}$
- System Keys. $\boxed{\text{y}}$

Text Editing Property Sheet

When you select the Text Editing property sheet, the following default key bindings are displayed:

- Delete Character Forward. $\boxed{\textbf{DELETE}}$
- Delete Character Backward. $\boxed{\textbf{BACKSPACE}}$
- Delete Word Forward. $\boxed{\textbf{SHIFT}}$ $\boxed{\textbf{CTRL}}$ $\boxed{\textbf{DELETE}}$
- Delete Word Backward. $\boxed{\textbf{SHIFT}}$ $\boxed{\textbf{CTRL}}$ $\boxed{\textbf{BACKSPACE}}$
- Delete Line Forward. $\boxed{\textbf{CTRL}}$ $\boxed{\textbf{DELETE}}$
- Delete Line Backward. $\boxed{\textbf{CTRL}}$ $\boxed{\textbf{BACKSPACE}}$
- Delete Line $\boxed{\textbf{SHIFT}}$ $\boxed{\textbf{ALT}}$ $\boxed{\textbf{DELETE}}$

Navigation Property Sheet

When you select the Navigation property sheet, the following default key bindings are displayed.

- Next Field. $\boxed{\textbf{TAB}}$ or $\boxed{\textbf{CTRL}}$ $\boxed{\textbf{TAB}}$
- Prev Field. $\boxed{\textbf{SHIFT}}$ $\boxed{\textbf{TAB}}$ or $\boxed{\textbf{SHIFT}}$ $\boxed{\textbf{CTRL}}$ $\boxed{\textbf{TAB}}$
- Up. $\boxed{\textbf{UP}}$
- Down. $\boxed{\textbf{DOWN}}$
- Left. $\boxed{\textbf{LEFT}}$
- Right. $\boxed{\textbf{RIGHT}}$
- Next Window. $\boxed{\textbf{ALT}}$ $\boxed{\textbf{F6}}$
- Previous Window. $\boxed{\textbf{SHIFT}}$ $\boxed{\textbf{ALT}}$ $\boxed{\textbf{F6}}$

- Next Application. `ALT` `ESC`
- Previous Application. `SHIFT` `ALT` `ESC`
- WordForward. `CTRL` `RIGHT`
- WordBackward. `CTRL` `LEFT`
- Line Start. `HOME`
- Line End. `END`
- Pane Start. `SHIFT` `CTRL` `HOME`
- Pane End. `SHIFT` `CTRL` `END`
- Document Start. `CTRL` `HOME`
- Document End. `CTRL` `END`

Scrolling Property Sheet

When you access the Scrolling property sheet, the following default key bindings are displayed.

- Scroll Up. `PAGEUP`
- Scroll Down. `PAGEDOWN`
- Page Up. `CTRL` `PAGEUP`
- Page Down. `CTRL` `PAGEDOWN`
- Page Left. `CTRL` `[`
- Page Right `CTRL` `]`
- Scroll Left. `ALT` `[`
- Scroll Right. `ALT` `]`
- Scroll Top. `ALT` `PAGEUP`
- Scroll Bottom. `ALT` `PAGEDOWN`
- Scroll Left Edge. `ALT` `{`
- Scroll Right Edge. `ALT` `}`

Text Selection Property Sheet

When you select the Text Selection property sheet, the following default key bindings are displayed.

■ Select Character Forward. (SHIFT) (RIGHT)

■ Select Word Forward. (SHIFT) (CTRL) (RIGHT)

■ Select Line Forward. (SHIFT) (END)

■ Select Character Backward. (SHIFT) (LEFT)

■ Select Word Backward. (SHIFT) (CTRL) (LEFT)

■ Select Line Backward. (SHIFT) (HOME)

■ Select Line. (CTRL) (ALT) (LEFT)

■ Flip Selection Ends. (ALT) (INSERT)

Mouse Functions Property Sheet

When you select the se Functions property sheet, the following default key bindings are displayed.

■ Select. (spacebar) or (CTRL) (UP)

■ Adjust. (CTRL) (&)

■ Menu. (CTRL) (m), (F4)

■ Drag (F5)

■ Drop (F2)

Modifiers

■ Duplicate. (CTRL) (SPACE)

■ Set Menu Default. (SHIFT) (CTRL) (m) or (SHIFT) (F4)

Keyboard System Functions Property Sheet

When you select the System Functions property sheet, the following screen is displayed:

Figure 5-6: Keyboard System Functions Property Sheet

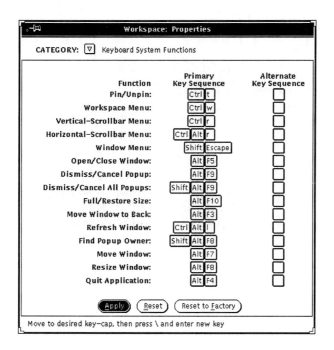

The default key bindings for the Keyboard System Functions property sheet are:

- Pin/Unpin. (CTRL) (t)
- Workspace Menu. (CTRL) (w)
- Window Menu. (SHIFT) (ESC)
- Vertical Scrollbar Menu. (CTRL) (r)
- Horizontal Scrollbar Menu. (CTRL) (ALT) (r)
- Open/Close Windows. (ALT) (F5)
- Dismiss/Cancel Popup. (ALT) (F9)
- Dismiss/Cancel All Popups. (SHIFT) (ALT) (F9)
- Full/Restore Size. (ALT) (F10)
- Move Window To Back. (ALT) (F3)
- Refresh Window. (CTRL) (ALT) (□)
- Find Popup Owner. (SHIFT) (ALT) (F8)
- Move Window. (ALT) (F7)
- Resize Window. (ALT) (F8)
- Quit Application. (ALT) (F4)

Miscellaneous Workspace Property Window

The Miscellaneous workspace property window defines the following settings:

- Beep. This defines when the system beep will sound. Choices are:
  - □ Always. The system will beep when notices and important footer messages appear on the screen.

□ Notices Only. The system will beep only when a notice appears on the screen.

□ Never. The system will not beep for any messages.

The default is "Always."

■ Window Layering. The choices are:

□ Individually. This means that when windows are moved to the back or front, each window (base and pop-up) is handled individually.

□ As a Group. This means that when a window is moved to the back or front, the entire window group (a base window and its associated pop-ups) moves. However, if a pop-up window is moved to the front or back, only the pop-up window moves.

The default is "As a Group."

■ Start OPEN LOOK GUI (Graphical User Interface) at Login. This is set to Yes or No to enable you to log into the OPEN LOOK Interface without having to type `olinit`. The default is "No."

If you change this option, the new value will be displayed on the property sheet, but will not take effect until you log out and then log in again.

■ SELECT Mouse Press. This determines whether the SELECT button should pop up a menu or invoke the menu default. Choices are:

□ Displays Default. This means that when you select a menu button, the default will execute. It is designed as a shortcut operation: when you set the menu default to the one you use most often, you can click SELECT on the menu
button and execute the action instead of having to click MENU, wait for the MENU to come up, and then select the item from the menu.

If you are using a keyboard, press ⎡**spacebar**⎤ on the selected menu button.

If you press SELECT on a menu button or item, the default will be displayed.

        ☐ Displays Menu. This means that if you select a menu button, the menu is displayed. SELECT functions the same way on a menu button as MENU; you drag to the item of your choice, and release SELECT to execute it.

        The default is "Displays Menu."

- Help Model. If you select the Input Focus option, you can move input focus to the item with which you need help and then press the ⟨F1⟩ key. If you select the Pointer option, you can position the mouse pointer on any item and then press ⟨F1⟩ to get help.

- Set Input Area. There are two settings for this option:

        ☐ You can click SELECT on a window to move input focus to it.

        ☐ You can simply move the pointer to another window in order to move input focus to it, without having to click SELECT.

- Interface Appearance. Two options are provided:

        ☐ 2D

        ☐ 3D

The 3D option is not available on monochrome monitors. The default for this feature is 2D visuals on monochrome systems and 3D on color and grayscale systems. Controls on a white or black background will appear two- dimensional, regardless of the color setting.

- Mnemonics Appearance. Allows you to specify how mnemonics are to be displayed, the mnemonic key name for a particular control, and whether to turn mnemonics on or off. The default is On - Underline.

        ☐ Off

        ☐ On - Underline

        ☐ On - Highlight

        ☐ On - Don't Show

If you choose not to display the mnemonic, you can choose the On - Don't Show option. If you choose the Highlight option, the mnemonic characters will be displayed in inverse video. Controls with glyphs as labels are not required to display the mnemonic.

■ Accelerators. Allows you to specify whether accelerators are to be displayed, and turn accelerators on and off. The default is On - Show.

   □ Off

   □ On - Show

   □ On - Don't Show

If you choose the Show option, accelerators will be displayed to the right of the control label or caption; multiple key sequences will be displayed with a "+" between the keys.

Figure 5-7 shows the Miscellaneous workspace property window.

Figure 5-7: Miscellaneous Workspace Property Window

```
┌──────────────────────────────────────────────────────────────────┐
│ ⚬           Workspace: Properties                                  │
│                                                                    │
│   CATEGORY: [▽] Miscellaneous                                      │
│  ┌──────────────────────────────────────────────────────────────┐ │
│  │                                                                │ │
│  │                 Beep: │Always│ Notices Only │ Never │          │ │
│  │       Window Layering: │ Individually │ As a Group │           │ │
│  │  Start OPEN LOOK GUI at login: │ Yes │ No │                    │ │
│  │     SELECT Mouse Press: │ Displays Default │ Displays Menu │    │ │
│  │           Help Model: │ Input Focus │ Pointer │                │ │
│  │        Set Input Area: │ Click SELECT │ Move Pointer │         │ │
│  │   Interface Appearance: │ 2D │ 3D │                            │ │
│  │          Mnemonics: │ Off │ On- Underline │ On- Highlight │ On- Don't Show │ │
│  │         Accelerators: │ Off │ On- Show │ On- Don't Show │      │ │
│  │                                                                │ │
│  │          ( Apply )   ( Reset )   ( Reset to Factory )          │ │
│  │                                                                │ │
│  └──────────────────────────────────────────────────────────────┘ │
│                                                                    │
└──────────────────────────────────────────────────────────────────┘
```

6 The File Manager Application

Introduction

The File Manager application is an independent OPEN LOOK client application that enables you to view and manipulate the UNIX file system without leaving the OPEN LOOK Interface.

The File Manager application enables you to do these UNIX System functions without typing a single UNIX command:

- View all of your files and directories.

- Create new files or directories.

- Copy, link, or rename files or directories.

- Delete files or directories.

- Perform file-specific actions such as executing, editing, or printing.

- Change ownership, access and modification time, or permissions for files or directories.

- Customize the display for many different views of your files.

- Browse the file system from other OPEN LOOK clients.

Organization of the Chapter

The contents of this chapter are arranged as follows:

- Accessing the File Manager Application.

  Explains how to use the mouse buttons in the File Manager application, and how to create a File Manager window from the Workspace menu. Describes File Manager application features, including the elements of the File Manager window, and the control panel and its buttons.

- Using the File Manager Application.

  Explains how to perform different functions with the File, View, and Edit menu buttons, and their menus.

Using the Mouse

Each mouse button performs a specific function in the File Manager application, as shown in Figure 6-1. Refer to the section, "Using the Mouse," in Chapter 2, for detailed information on using the mouse buttons.

Figure 6-1: Mouse Button Functions

Use This Mouse Button	Located	To Perform This Function
SELECT	On the left	Select objects or manipulate controls.
ADJUST	In the middle	Toggle the state of an object to select or unselect.
MENU	On the right	Display and select menu items.

The SELECT Button

Use the SELECT button to select a directory entry. You must select at least one object — file or directory — from the directory pane in order to perform the Open, Copy, Link, Move, or Print commands from the file menu, or the Delete and File Properties functions from the Edit menu. The menus are described in the section, "Using the File Manager Application."

The ADJUST Button

The ADJUST button has two functions in the File Manager application. It enables you to select multiple objects to perform a common function. For example, if you want to perform the same menu action on two or more objects, you can move the pointer to the first object and click SELECT. Then move the pointer to a second object and click ADJUST. This expands the set of selected objects. Do this with any number of objects until you are ready to make a choice from the menu.

The ADJUST button also toggles the selected state of an entry, from selected to unselected and back again.

The MENU Button

Use the MENU button to display menus on the control area, path pane, or directory pane and to select entries on any of the menus.

Using the Keyboard

OPEN LOOK allows you to perform File Manager operations using the keyboard instead of, or in combination with, a mouse. In order to manipulate files without a mouse, you will use the three methods listed below. See "Using the Keyboard" in Chapter 2 for a description of each method.

- Keyboard navigation

- Mnemonics

- Accelerators

Keyboard Navigation

The File Manager supports the use of the navigation keys ⬆, ⬇, ⬅, and ➡ to move between glyphs (graphic representations of directories & files) within a pane.

To manipulate a particular object, navigate to the desired object using one of the navigation keys, and do the following:

1. Select the object by pressing [**spacebar**]. (Modify selections by using [**CTRL**] [**&**]). Press [**ALT**] [**m**] to bring up a menu.

2. Use the appropriate mnemonic to perform the desired action from the menu.

Using the Text Fields

Some of the File Manager functions depend on your keyboard input in text fields. Refer to the subsection "Using Text Fields" in Chapter 4 for more details, but the following guidelines should enable you to type into a File Manager text field:

■ Position the pointer on the text field exactly where you intend to type or insert new text. This can be at the beginning of a blank line, or at any point on a line that already has text in it.

■ Click SELECT on the text field to give it active input focus. The small triangle, the caret, jumps to the space you have selected. You can type to insert text here.

■ Although the File Manager text fields may appear to be too short for the amount of text you want to type, you can actually type as many as 1,000 characters into any of them. When the field contains more text than it can show, the field scrolls to accommodate the text.

■ Press (**BACKSPACE**) to delete. If you want to delete characters from text that is already in place, move the pointer to the immediate right of the character you want to delete and click SELECT to place the caret on that spot. Use the (**BACKSPACE**) to delete characters behind the caret.

■ To delete larger amounts of text, you can "sweep" by pressing SELECT and dragging across the text to be deleted. This action deletes the text as you type new data into the space.

■ To delete the entire line of text, place the caret at the beginning of the line and press (**CTRL**) (**DELETE**).

Accessing the File Manager Application

Access the File Manager application through the workspace menu with the following procedure:

MOUSE:

1. Access the workspace menu by pressing or clicking MENU on the workspace area. See the section "Operating on Menus" in Chapter 4 for details on menu access.

2. Drag the pointer to Utilities.

    Continue to drag the pointer to the arrow to the right for the Utilities submenu. The following choices are displayed:

    - File Manager

    - Network Administration

    - Refresh

    - Print Screen

3. Release the MENU button on the File Manager choice on the Utilities submenu.

KEYBD:

1. Press (CTRL) (w) to bring up the workspace menu.

2. Use the (↓) to move the highlighting to the Utilities option.

3. Press (→) to display the submenu.

    The following choices are displayed:

    - File Manager

    - Network Administration

    - Refresh

    - Print Screen

4. Type (f) to access the File Manager window.

Use this procedure to create one or more File Manager base windows.

You can also achieve access to the File Manager application through other OPEN LOOK Interface client applications,such as the Pixmap Editor, which offers a Browse window button.

File Manager Features

The File Manager base window displays your working directory with graphic representations, called glyphs, of the directories, files, and executables in your UNIX file system. Two sub-panes display your path in detail: the path pane, which shows the directory you are in, and the directory pane, which shows all files, directories, and executables within your current working directory.

Figure 6-2 shows the File Manager base window.

Figure 6-2: The File Manager Base Window

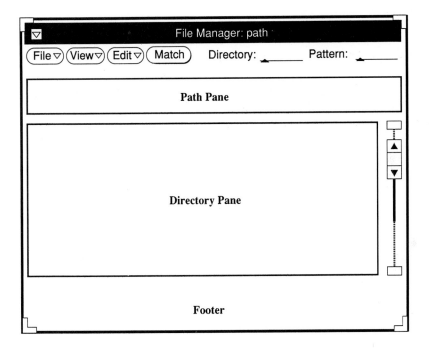

The File Manager base window contains the following elements:

- Title: The current path name
- Scrollbars, if needed, on both the path pane and directory pane
- File menu button
- View menu button
- Edit menu button

- Match button. This command button is used with the two text fields. When you type the path in one or both text fields, you select Match to activate the file search and change to that path.

- Two text fields:

  □ Directory. Change directories by entering a new path in this field.

  □ Pattern. Enter a pattern in this field to limit the display to files that match the pattern and all directories in the path.

- Pane. The pane displays the current user view. The pane area is divided into two sub-panes:

  □ Path pane. The path pane contains a graphic representation of the current path. Each directory is represented by a glyph and the directory name. The root directory is named "/."

  □ Directory pane. The directory pane contains a list of the directories and files in your current path. A vertical and/or horizontal scrollbar is beside the pane if the content of the directory pane requires scrolling. Each entry in the pane is displayed with a representative glyph. The File Manager application uses the following standard types of glyphs:

Figure 6-3: Types of File Manager Glyphs

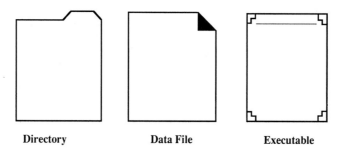

| Directory | Data File | Executable |

The File Manager also provides the following additional glyphs.

Figure 6-4: Additional File Manager Glyphs

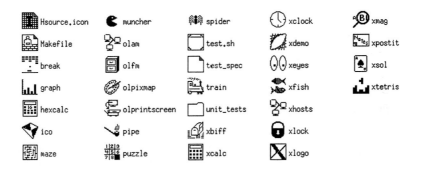

Using the File Manager Application

You can perform all File Manager functions through the controls in the control area, using the File, View, and Edit menus to operate on files and directories, and the text fields and Match button to change your path.

The Open Function

The Open function appears on several menus within the File Manager application. Open causes the File Manager application to execute the default action for the selected object, which can be a file, directory, or executable.

The default action is the action that the file is programmed to execute. It is determined by the system (called the factory default), or by the installer or system administrator and set by changing the binding file, .olfmrc.

The binding file defines types and associates attributes with those types. Attributes include glyphs, Open command defaults, the Print command, and pop-up menus. Factory defaults are supplied by the OPEN LOOK Interface and already defined in the binding file but may be changed by a programmer or experienced user.

The typical OPEN LOOK user will probably never have cause to change the defaults in the binding file. Appendix C, "File Manager Application: Binding File," contains programmer's information on the .olfmrc file.

The glyphs associated with the objects in the directory pane identify their default actions. The following describes the default actions for some of the objects in the directory pane:

- The default action of a Directory is to cd (change the working directory) to that directory. This means that if you select a directory and then select Open from the file menu, the working directory will change to the selected directory and the directory pane will be updated.

- A Data File runs the default editor. This means that if you select a data file and then select Open from the file menu, the selected file will appear in a Terminal Emulator window ready to be edited with your default editor.

- An Executable executes an action. This means that if you select an executable program and then select Open from the file menu, a Terminal Emulator window will pop up and initiate the execution in the background.

There are several ways you can open, or select the default, of an object. Each object has an associated pop-up menu, attainable by pressing or clicking MENU on the object. You can select Open on the pop-up menu. You can double-click SELECT on the selected object. You can use the "drag and drop" procedure, described in the subsection "Drag and Drop" on page 40.

Changing the Path

The File Manager application provides several ways in which you can move through the UNIX file system. Follow these steps to move to a new directory:

MOUSE:

1. Double-click SELECT on a directory glyph in either the path pane or directory pane,

— or —

2. Select the directory you want to change to and select Open from the File menu,

— or —

3. Press MENU on the new directory and select Open from the directory or path pop-up menu,

KEYBD:

1. Press (**TAB**) until the highlighting moves to the pane from which you want to perform the operation.

2. Use the (↑), (↓), (←), and (→) keys to move input focus to the desired directory.

3. Press (**CTRL**) (**m**) to display the directory pop-up menu.

4. Press (**o**) to open the directory.

— or —

5. Press (**TAB**) until the highlighting moves to the window from which you want to perform the operation.

6. Use the ⬆, ⬇, ⬅, and ➡ keys to move input focus to the desired directory.

7. Press **spacebar** twice on the directory.

Using the Text Fields and Match Button to Change Directories

You can change the current path by using one or both of the two text fields in the control panel at the top of the File Manager window. To do this, you:

- Type the name of the directory you want in the text field "Directory." Refer to the subsection, "Using the Text Fields," in "Accessing the File Manager Application," in this chapter for information on typing into a text field.

- If you want to specify a matching pattern, type that in the "Pattern" text field. For example, if you want to see only files that begin with the letter "L," you type L* in the "Pattern" text field.

  * matches any character or group of characters, while ? matches any single character.

Press Match after either or both of the above steps.

If you specify a matching pattern, the directory pane will change to reflect the files and directories that match your pattern.

If you press ⏎ after entering text in these fields, the Match action will automatically be initiated.

The File Menu Button

The file menu button is the first menu button on the File Manager control pane. The file menu gives you Open, Move, Copy, Link, Print, and Create functions. Edit functions are performed with Open (which opens an existing file), or Create File (which opens a new file with the default editor).

The file menu contains the following items:

- Open
- Copy
- Link
- Move
- Print
- Create Directory
- Create File

Open, Copy, Move, Link, and Print operate on selected object(s), such as files or directories. If no files or directories are selected, the Open, Move, Copy, Link, and Print items dim to show that they are deactivated. Once you select one or more files or directories from the directory pane, these items become activated again. If you select more than one object, Open becomes deactivated, since you can open only one object at a time.

Figure 6-5 shows the file menu.

Figure 6-5: The File Menu

To apply any of the functions on the file menu:

MOUSE:

1. Select one or more files or directories. To do this,

    – Move the pointer to a file or directory and click SELECT.

    – Move the pointer to a second file or directory and click ADJUST.
      Do this with any number of objects until you are ready to make
      a selection from the file menu.

2. Press MENU on the File menu button.

3. Drag the pointer to the function you wish to perform and release MENU.

KEYBD:

1. Press ⌈**TAB**⌉ to move the highlighting to the desired pane.

2. Use the ⌈↑⌉, ⌈↓⌉, ⌈←⌉, and ⌈→⌉ keys to move to different objects within
   the pane.

3. Press ⌈**spacebar**⌉ to select the file or directory.

4. To select another file or directory, move input focus to the desired item
   and press ⌈**CTRL**⌉ ⌈**&.**⌉

5. Press ⌈**TAB**⌉ until the File menu button in the control pane is selected.

6. Press ⌈**CTRL**⌉ ⌈**m**⌉.

7. Type the mnemonic that corresponds to the function you want to perform.

Open

The Open item on the file menu performs the following default actions according to the object upon which it is applied:

■ Data file is placed in a default editor

■ Changes to a directory

■ Executes an action on an executable program

To avoid overloading the system, Open must operate on one object at a time.
When multiple objects are selected in the directory pane, Open is deactivated in
the File menu.

Copy

The Copy function copies files and directories in the following ways:

■ Copy a file into the same directory by giving the file another name.

■ Copy a directory and its contents by giving the directory another name.

■ Copy one or more file(s) into a new directory. The File Manager application creates a directory of the name you supply and copies the file or files
with their original names into the directory.

■ Copy one or more file(s) into an existing directory. The File Manager
application copies the file or files into the directory you specify, keeping
their names if no other such names exist, or displaying a warning notice
that reads *<Filename>* exists. Overwrite? if the name already exists.

The Copy window item on the file menu invokes the Copy command window,
as shown in Figure 6-6. You use this Copy command window to perform the
above-mentioned copying functions.

Figure 6-6: The Copy Command Window

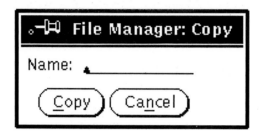

The Copy command window has the following elements:

- Text field. Here you enter the name of the file or directory into which you want to copy the selection.

- Copy. Select this button when you have selected and entered the destination of the files or directories you want to copy.

- Cancel. Select this button to cancel proceedings.

As file or directory copy procedures begin, the following status information is displayed:

    Press STOP to abort operation: Copying file <*filename*>.

When the operation is completed, the following message is displayed:

    Copy completed. Use Undo to remove copy.

If you press `CTRL` `s` during the Copy procedure, the following message is displayed:

    Copy cancelled.

You can still undo the action with the Undo item on the edit menu, as long as you have not performed another action. See the subsection, "Edit Menu Button," for information on the Undo procedure.

The following table shows what action the Copy command performs depending on what you enter in the "Name" text field. Note that in addition to the regular UNIX System restrictions, an invalid file name is one with more than 14 characters. (However this convention is operating system dependent. Some operating systems allow more than 14 characters.)

Figure 6-7: Copy Command Window Actions

	Action Performed On	
Your Input	Single Selection	Multiple Selection
New file or directory name	The selected file or directory is copied to the new file or directory name.	A new directory is created and the selected files are copied into it.
An existing file name	Select Overwrite to delete the old file and overwrite the selected file to the existing name. Select Skip to cancel the copy procedure.	A notice that reads, *<Filename>* exists. Overwrite? appears on the window. Select Overwrite to delete the old file and overwrite the selected file to a new directory with the existing name. Select Skip to cancel copying procedures on only the file with the existing name.
An existing directory name	The selected file is copied into the directory, if there is no other file of that name already existing in the directory. If a file with the same name exists, a notice that reads, *<Filename>* exists. Overwrite? appears on the	The selected files are copied into the directory, if there are no other files of the same names already existing in the directory. If a file with the same name exists, a notice that reads, *<Filename>* exists. Overwrite?

Figure 6-7: Copy Command Window Actions (continued)

| | Action Performed On | |
Your Input	Single Selection	Multiple Selection
	window. Using either the mouse or the keyboard, select Overwrite to delete the old file and overwrite the selected file to the existing name. Select Skip to cancel the copy procedure.	appears on the window. Select Overwrite to delete the old file and overwrite the selected file to the existing name. Select Skip to cancel the copy procedure.
An invalid name	An error message appears in the File Manager base window footer and you are prompted for a valid entry.	An error message appears in the File Manager base window footer and you are prompted for a valid entry.

 NOTE Remember that you can't copy an object to itself.

Move

The Move function moves files in the following ways:

- Rename a file or directory.

- Move a file into a new directory with a new or same name.

- Move a directory and its contents to another directory.

- Move more than one file into a new directory. The File Manager application creates a directory of the name you supply and moves the files with their original names into the directory.

- Move more than one file into an existing directory. The File Manager application moves the files into the directory you specify, keeping their names if no other such names exist, or displaying a warning notice that reads `Overwrite?` if the name already exists.

The Move window item on the file menu invokes the Move command window, as shown in Figure 6-8. You use this Move command window to perform the above-mentioned moving functions.

Figure 6-8: The Move Command Window

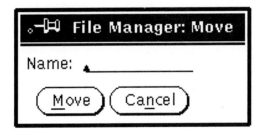

The Move command window has the following elements:

- Text field. Here you enter the name of the directory into which you want to move the selection.
- Move. Select this button when you are ready to start the Move proceedings.
- Cancel. Select this button to cancel proceedings.

As move procedures begin, the following status information appears:

> `Press STOP to abort operation: Moving file <`*filename*`>.`

When the operation is completed, the following message appears:

> `Move completed.  Use Undo to restore file/directory to former`
> `location.`

You can undo the action with the Undo item on the edit menu as long as you have not performed another action. See the subsection, "Edit Menu Button," for information on the Undo procedure.

If you press ⎡**CTRL**⎤ ⎡**s**⎤ during the operation, the following message is displayed:

> `Move cancelled.`

The following table shows what action the Move command performs depending on what you enter in the Name text field. Note that in addition to the regular UNIX System restrictions, an invalid file name is one with more than 14 characters. (However, this convention is operating system dependent. Some operating systems allow file names to have more than 14 characters.)

Figure 6-9: Move Command Window Actions

	Action Performed On	
Your Input	Single Selection	Multiple Selection
New directory name	The selected file is moved to the new directory.	A new directory is created and the selected files are moved into it.
An existing directory name	The selected file or directory is moved into the directory. If you are moving a directory and there is another directory of that name already existing, the contents of the selected directory are added to the directory you type in the	The selected files are moved into the directory, if there are no other files of the same names already existing in the directory. If a notice that reads, `<`*Filename*`> exists. Overwrite?` appears on the window, select the

Figure 6-9: Move Command Window Actions (continued)

Your Input	Action Performed On	
	Single Selection	Multiple Selection
	text field. If a file of the same name exists, a notice that reads, *<Filename>* exists. Overwrite? appears on the window. Using either the mouse or the keyboard, select the Overwrite button to delete the old file and overwrite the selected file to the existing name. Select the Skip button to cancel move procedures on only the file with the existing name.	Overwrite button to delete the old file and overwrite the selected file to the existing name. Select the Skip button to cancel move procedures on only the file with the existing name.
An invalid name	An error message appears in the File Manager base window footer and you are prompted for a valid entry.	An error message appears in the File Manager base window footer and you are prompted for a valid entry.
An existing file name (not a directory)	The selected file or directory replaces the existing file, which is deleted. A notice that reads *<Filename>* exists. Overwrite? appears on the window. Using either the keyboard or the mouse, select the Overwrite button to delete the existing file and overwrite the	The selected files are copied into a new directory that replaces the existing file. A notice that reads *<Filename>* exists. Overwrite? appears in the window. Using either the keyboard or the mouse, select the Overwrite button to delete the existing file and overwrite the

Figure 6-9: Move Command Window Actions (continued)

Your Input	Action Performed On	
	Single Selection	Multiple Selection
	selected file to the existing name. Select the Skip button to cancel the move procedure on the selected file.	selected file to a new directory with the name of the previously existing file. Select the Skip button to cancel the move procedure on all the selected files.

NOTE Remember that you can't move an object to itself.

Link

The Link function links the same file to more than one destination. For example, you can link a file to another directory using this command, and although only one copy exists of the file, it will be listed in and be accessible from both directories. You can give the file the same or another name, but it is still the same file — when you make changes to the file in one directory, you will see these changes no matter what directory you are in when you bring it up.

NOTE You cannot link across *file systems* unless you are using UNIX System V Release 4.0.

The Link window item on the file menu invokes the Link command window, as shown in Figure 6-10.

Figure 6-10: Link Command Window

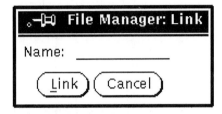

The Link command window has the following elements:

- Text field. Here you enter the name of the directory into which you want to link the selection.

- Link button. Select this button when you are ready to start the Link proceedings.

- Cancel button. Select this button to cancel proceedings.

As link procedures begin, the following status information appears:

    Press STOP to abort operation: Linking file <*filename*>.

When the operation is completed, the following message appears:

    Link completed. Use Undo to remove link.

You can undo the action with the Undo item from the edit menu, as long as you have not performed another action. See the subsection, "Edit Menu Button," for information on the Undo procedure.

Figure 6-11 shows what action the Link command performs depending on what you enter in the "Name" text field. Note that in addition to the regular UNIX System restrictions, an invalid file name is one with more than 14 characters. (However, this convention is operating system dependent. Some operating systems allow files that have more than 14 characters.)

Figure 6-11: Link Command Window Actions

Your Input	Action Performed On	
	Single Selection	Multiple Selection
New file name	The selected file is linked to the new file.	A new directory with the new file name is created and the selected files are linked into it.
An existing file name	A notice that reads, *<Filename>* exists. Overwrite? appears on the window. Using either the mouse or the keyboard, select Overwrite to delete the old file and overwrite the selected file to the existing name. Select Skip to cancel procedures. You will be reprompted for the target name.	A notice that reads, *<Filename>* exists. Overwrite? appears on the window. Using either a keyboard or a mouse, select Overwrite to delete the old file and create a new directory with the selected files linked into it. Select Skip to cancel procedures. You will be reprompted for the target name.
An existing directory name	The selected file is linked into the directory, if there is no other file of that name already existing in the directory. If a file with the same name exists, a notice that reads, *<Filename>* exists. Overwrite? appears on the window. Using either the mouse or the keyboard, select Overwrite to delete the old file and overwrite the selected file to the existing name. Select Skip to cancel procedures. You will be	The selected files are copied into the directory, if there are no other files of the same names already existing in the directory. If a file with the same name exists, a notice that reads, *<Filename>* exists. Overwrite? appears on the window. Using either the mouse or the keyboard, select Overwrite to delete the old file and create a new directory with the selected files linked into it. Select Skip to cancel pro-

Figure 6-11: Link Command Window Actions (continued)

	Action Performed On	
Your Input	Single Selection	Multiple Selection
	reprompted for the target name.	cedures. You will be reprompted for the target name.
An invalid name	An error message appears in the File Manager base window footer and you are prompted for a valid entry.	An error message appears in the File Manager base window footer and you are prompted for a valid entry.
The name of the directory you are currently in, or an existing file name in the same directory	An error message appears in the File Manager base window footer to inform you that no action is required.	An error message appears in the File Manager base window footer to inform you that no action is required.

Print

The Print command item causes the File Manager application to execute the print command to send the selected files to your default printer destination. Your system administrator or installer should tell you what the print command is for your site.

Create Directory

The Create Directory window item supplies you with a window with a text field in which you type the name of the directory you wish to create. There are two buttons on this window:

- Create Directory. This button creates the directory you name.

■ Cancel. This button cancels proceedings.

Errors are reported in the footer of the base window. When refreshed, the directory pane will reflect this addition.

Create File

The Create window item supplies you with a window with a text field in which you type the name of the file you wish to create. To create a file within your working directory, simply type the new file name. To create a file in another directory, type the path name including the directory in which you wish to create it.

There are two buttons on the Create File window:

■ Create File. Select this button once you type the name of the new file. The File Manager application runs the default editor and produces a Terminal Emulator window in which you can enter your file data. The editor is either the one specified in the $EDITOR environment variable or vi (if the variable is not set).

■ Cancel. This button cancels proceedings.

Errors are reported in the footer of the base window. The directory does not reflect the addition until the next update.

View Menu Button

The View menu button is the second menu button on the File Manager control panel. You press MENU or (CTRL) (m) on the View menu button to access the View selection pop-up menu. This menu contains the following items. You select any one of the following three, each of which gives you a different view of the pane display:

■ Sort

■ Detail

■ Order

Figure 6-12 shows the view menu.

Figure 6-12: The View Menu

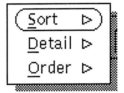

Sort

The Sort menu item on the view menu invokes the sort selection menu, as shown in Figure 6-13.

Figure 6-13: The Sort Selection Menu

You use the sort menu to select the sort order of your objects as follows:

■ Name. Select this item to list the files and directories in alphabetical order. This is the default selection.

■ Newest. Select this item to list the files and directories by the order of most recently modified to first modified.

■ Oldest. Select this item to list the files and directories by the order of first modified to most recently modified.

■ Largest. Select this item to list the files and directories in order of largest-sized file first to smallest-sized file last.

■ Smallest. Select this item to list the files and directories in order of smallest-sized file first to largest-sized file last.

■ Type. Select this item to list the files and directories grouped by the glyphs that identify them.

Detail

The Detail menu button on the view menu invokes the detail selection menu, as shown in Figure 6-14.

Figure 6-14: The Detail Selection Menu

Detail selection determines how the objects in your current directory will be displayed. You use the detail menu to select the format for the display in the pane, as follows:

■ Name. Select this item to list the objects with name and glyph only. This is the default selection.

■ Brief. Select this item to list the files and directories with all the above information (Name), plus the object size, permissions, dates and times of modification.

■ Full. Select this item to list the files and directories with all of the above information (Brief) plus the owner and group names.

Order

The Order menu item on the view menu invokes the order selection menu, as shown in Figure 6-15.

Figure 6-15: The Order Selection Menu

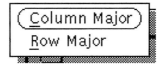

You use the order menu to select the format for horizontal or vertical display of your objects, as follows:

- Column Major. Select this item to list the objects in columns (vertical by sort order). This is effective only when multiple columns are displayed. Column Major is the default selection.

- Row Major. Select this item to list the objects in rows (horizontal by sort order).

Edit Menu Button

The Edit menu button is the third menu button on the File Manager control panel. This menu button provides a menu from which you select functions that perform miscellaneous file management activities.

NOTE Editing files is not one of the activities included on the edit menu. You use the Open item or the Create File item on the file menu to edit a file. You can also edit a file by pressing MENU on any individual editable file in the directory pane and selecting Open from that directory pane menu. See the subsection, "Directory Pane Menu" later in this section for details.

When you press MENU or press (**CTRL**) (**m**) on the Edit menu button, you access the edit selection pop-up menu.

The edit menu contains the following items:

- Select All
- Delete
- File Properties
- Properties
- Undo

To select from the Edit menu, drag the pointer and release at the item of your choice.

Figure 6-16 shows the Edit menu.

Figure 6-16: The Edit Menu

Select All

The Select All item on the edit menu enables you to select all of the objects in
the Directory pane in order to perform a common function on all files and directories.

Delete

Select Delete to remove the selected file or directory from the system. As delete
procedures begin, the following status information is displayed:

> Press STOP to abort operation.   Deleting <*filename*>.

When the operation is completed, the following message is displayed:

> Deletion completed. Use Undo to restore file/directory.

If you press ⟨**CTRL**⟩ ⟨**s**⟩, before the operation is completed, the following message is displayed:

> Delete cancelled.

You can still retrieve the deleted file by selecting Undo, as long as you have not
performed another action.

File Properties

The Properties window item invokes the file properties command window
shown in Figure 6-17. This window is used to change the filename, owner,
group, access time, modification time and permissions on a file or directory.

The File Properties command window has the following elements:

- Text fields. You enter the file name, owner, and group of the file for
  which you wish to change permissions.

  If you do not own the selected file, then all but the Name field will be
  inactive. If you do not even have Write permission, then the Name field
  will be inactive as well.

  Access Time and Modification Time: The text fields for Access Time and
  Modification Time will initially display the original access and
  modification times on the selected file. If you want to change the
  access/modification time to the current time in the format *mm/dd/yy* and
  hh:mm, then you have to delete the existing time(s) from both the date and
  time fields. If you want to change the access and/or modification time to

a specific time, then you must type the new time in the *mm/dd/yy* format in the first field (the date field), and the *hh:mm* format in the second field (the time field). A change in the modification time will automatically be reflected in the access time fields. Select Apply to initiate the action. Select Reset to return to the original times.

 NOTE The earliest date you can set is 01/01/70. If you set a date earlier than that, the system will automatically change the date to 01/01/70. Similarly, the latest date you can set is 01/18/2038. If you indicate a year not in this century, you must type the year as 20yy; typing only 38 defaults to 1938.

■ Nonexclusive settings. You can select Read, Write, or Execute to change one or all of owner access, group access, or other access permissions.

■ Apply. Select this button to incorporate your changes.

■ Reset. Select this button to return to the previously applied properties.

Figure 6-17: File Properties: Command Window

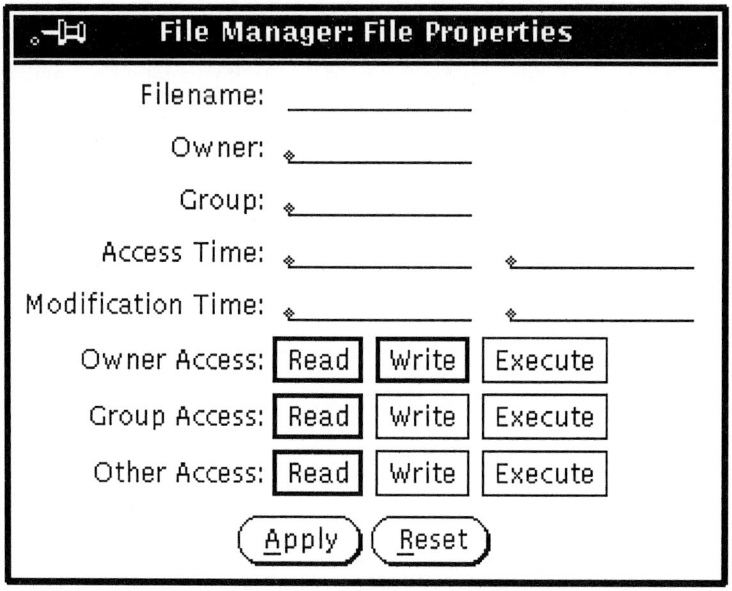

Properties

The Properties menu item on the edit menu invokes the File Manager property window with which you can customize the defaults of the File Manager. The File Manager property window is shown in Figure 6-18.

The File Manager property window has controls with which you can customize settings for the following attributes.

- Sort. The factory default is "Name." You can change it to any of the available Sort choices. Refer to the subsection "Sort" under "View Menu Button" for more information on the choices.

- Detail. The factory default is "Name." You can change it to any of the available Detail choices. Refer to the subsection "Detail" under "View Menu Button" for more information on the choices.

- Order. The factory default is "Column Major." You can change it to the other choice, "Row Major." Refer to the subsection "Order" under "View Menu Button" for more information on the choices.

- Show Hidden Files. This setting gives you the option of showing the files, such as .profile, which are not normally listed because they begin with a "." The factory default is "No."

- Notice On Delete. This setting gives you the option of receiving or not receiving a notice verification when you delete a file. The factory default is "Yes."

- Update Timer. This setting determines how often the system checks for changes you have made to the data within the File Manager application, including changes made from other applications. "Sometimes" checks every 90 seconds, "Often" checks every 30 seconds. The default is "sometimes."

- Undo. This setting has a choice of two exclusive settings: Enable and Disable. Select Disable to turn off the Undo feature (described on 37), so that files about to be deleted are not saved. Select Enable to reinstate the Undo feature.

Figure 6-18: File Manager: Properties

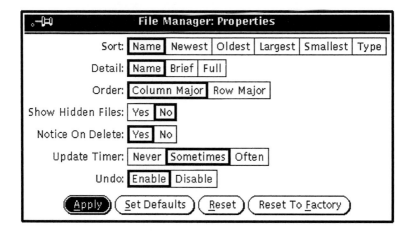

The buttons at the bottom of the window control affect the properties of the currently displayed File Manager base window. The buttons control the following functions:

■ Apply. Select this button to incorporate your final changes. The Apply button causes settings to take immediate effect on the File Manager base window.

■ Set Defaults. Select this button to permanently store your applied settings to be used in subsequent File Manager base windows. If you apply settings using this window, and select the Set Defaults button, then any other File Manager base windows you create subsequent to this will incorporate the settings you apply here. Any File Manager windows that already exist on the workspace will not be automatically changed to incorporate the new settings.

- Reset. Select this button to return the properties to the previously applied settings.

- Reset to Factory. Select this button to return the properties to the system settings.

Undo

The Undo item on the edit menu enables you to literally undo the Copy, Move, Link, Create Directory, and Delete actions. To use this function, do not perform any other action once you have done the Copy, Move, Link, Create Directory, or Delete function. Simply select Undo from the edit menu, and the file system will return to its state before you performed that function. For example, if you copy a file by using Copy on the file menu and then you decide that you did not want to copy that file, you can go to the edit menu and select Undo. The new copied file or files will disappear from the directory pane listing.

Using Menus in the Panes

Path Pane Menu

The path pane menu enables you to open and change properties of any directory you have selected. To access the path pane menu, do the following:

MOUSE:

1. Select a directory in the path pane.

2. Press MENU.

KEYBD:

1. Press (TAB) until the highlighting moves to the path pane.

2. Use the (↑), (↓), (←), and (→) keys to move the highlighting to the desired object.

3. Press CTRL   m .

The following menu is displayed:

Figure 6-19: Path Pane Menu

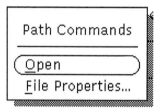

The path pane and the directory pane change to reflect the new current path. The items on the path pane menu do the following:

- Open. Select this command item to open, or cd, a directory. The directory's contents will be displayed in the panes.

- File Properties. Select this window item to change properties of a selected directory via a "File Properties" window. This is the same File Properties window found on the Edit Menu.

Directory Pane Menu

The directory pane menu enables you to perform actions on selected files. To access the directory pane menu:

MOUSE:

1. Position the pointer on any selected file within the pane display.

2. Press MENU.

KEYBD:

1. Press (**TAB**) until the highlighting moves to the directory pane.

2. Use the (↑), (↓), (←), and (→) keys to move the highlighting to a desired object.

3. Press (**CTRL**) (**m**).

The following menu is displayed:

Figure 6-20: Directory Pane Menu

The items on the directory pane menu are used for the following:

- Open. Select this command item to run the default operation; i.e., "edit" if it is an editable file, "execute" if it is an executable file.

- Delete. Select this command item to delete the selected file.

- File Properties. Select this window item to change the permissions of the selected file. This is the same File Properties window found on the Edit Menu.

- [For executable files only] If you have selected an executable file, the entry Edit File is added to the directory pane menu. This entry allows you to edit an executable shell script or .profile type file.

NOTE If you have selected a ".c" file, a Compile option appears on the menu.

Drag and Drop

With the "Drag and Drop" method of file system manipulation, you can use the pointer and mouse buttons to manipulate objects without typing in the text fields or using menus. When you drag an object to copy it, the pointer changes so that a glyph outline surrounds the pointer. To drop the object, you must make sure that the "hot spot," which is in the center of the outline at the tip of the arrow, lands on the destination object. Figure 6-21 shows the new form that the pointer takes for the Copy drag and drop procedure. You cannot move an object using the drag and drop procedure.

Figure 6-21: Copy Pointer

You can also perform the drag and drop copy function using the keyboard. See the next section, "Copy an Object," for information.

Copy an Object

The following procedure enables you to copy a file or other object from one
directory to another without having to select Copy from the file menu.

MOUSE:

1. Select an object by moving the pointer to the object of your choice and
   pressing SELECT, while dragging the object to another place on the
   screen. You will see an outline of the glyph that represents the object you
   are dragging.

2. "Drop" the object somewhere else: on another File Manager window, on
   the workspace, or on another application.

KEYBD:

1. Press (**TAB**) or (**SHIFT**) (**TAB**) to move the highlighting to the directory
   pane.

2. Use the (↑), (↓), (←), and (→) keys to move the highlighting to the
   desired object.

3. Press (**F5**) to drag the selected object to another location.

4. Use the (↑), (↓), (←), and (→) keys to move the "Copy" glyph to the
   desired location.

5. Press (**F2**) or (↵) to "drop" the object somewhere else: on another File
   Manager window, on the workspace, or on another application.

Change to a New Directory

Drag and drop a directory onto the workspace to bring up another File
Manager base window with the path in the selected directory.

Execute an Object or Edit a File

Drag and drop an executable file on the workspace to execute the object rather
than using Open on the file menu.

Drag and drop an editable file onto the workspace. A window labeled with
your default editor will be displayed and you can edit the file.

Operate Other Applications

Drag and drop any object on another client application to perform a client-determined function. For example, if you are running a mail application in a separate window, and you drag and drop a file from the File Manager application window to the mail application, the file is mailed. Refer to the documentation provided with your application to see if it supports this function.

The Browse Window

The File Manager provides a Browse window which can be accessed from the Pixmap application. If you select File from the Pixmap window, several choices are displayed. By selecting Browse, you can display a File Manager window that has all the functionality of the original File Manager window. The only difference is that the Browse File Window has a pushpin. For more information on the Browse window, refer to the olpixmap manual page in Appendix A.

Quick Reference Tables

The tables in this section are each contained to a page so you can remove them from the binder and keep them next to your computer for use as quick-reference cards.

The following table summarizes the functions you can perform from the different controls in the File Manager application.

File Manager Controls and their Functions

From the FILE button	From the VIEW button	From the EDIT button
OPEN	SORT: Name	SELECT ALL
COPY	Newest Oldest	DELETE
MOVE	Largest Smallest	FILE PROPERTIES
LINK	Type	PROPERTIES
PRINT		
CREATE DIRECTORY	DETAIL: Name	UNDO
CREATE FILE	Brief Full	
	ORDER: Column Major Row Major	

File Manager Application Commands

The following table summarizes the different ways in which you can use the File Manager application to perform UNIX System commands.

Edit an existing file (vi):	MOUSE: Press SELECT on the file glyph. Drag to the workspace and release SELECT. — or — Select a file from the directory pane, and then select Open from the file menu. — or — Press or click MENU on the file glyph and select Open from the directory pane menu. KEYBD: Press (TAB) until the file glyph highlights. Type (CTRL) (m). Type (o) to open the file.
Copy a file (cp):	MOUSE: Press SELECT on the file glyph. Drag to the same or another File Manager window and release on a directory glyph in that window. — or — Select a file from the directory pane, and then select Copy from the file menu. KEYBD: Press (TAB) until the desired pane highlights. Use the arrow keys to highlight the desired object. Press (F5) to begin the drag operation. Use the arrow keys to move the object to the desired location and press (F2) to drop the object.
Link a file (ln):	Select a file from the directory pane, and then select Link from the file menu.

File Manager Application Commands (continued)

Move a file (mv):	MOUSE: Select a file from the directory pane, and then select Move from the file menu. KEYBD: Press `TAB` to highlight the file glyph. Press `spacebar` to select the highlighted glyph. Press `TAB` until the File menu button is selected. Press `CTRL` `m`. Press `m` to begin the Move operation.
Create a new file:	Select Create File from the file menu.
Create a directory (mkdir):	Select Create Directory from the file menu.
Remove a file or directory (rm or rmdir) :	MOUSE: Select a file or directory, and then select Delete from the edit menu. — or — Press or click MENU on the file or directory glyph in the directory pane and select Delete from the directory pane menu. KEYBD: Press `TAB` to select a file or directory, and then select Delete from the edit menu.

File Manager Application Commands (continued)

Change working directory (cd):	MOUSE: Double-click on the directory glyph to change to that directory.
	— or —
	Select a directory, and then select Open from the file menu.
	— or —
	Press or click MENU on the directory glyph in either the path pane or directory and select Open from the path pane menu or directory pane menu.
	— or —
	Press SELECT on the directory glyph. Drag to the workspace and release SELECT. This will bring up another File Manager window with that directory.
	— or —
	Type in the text field the directory to which you want to change. Select the Match button.
	KEYBD: Press ⎡TAB⎤ to highlight a directory, and then select Open from the file menu.
Execute the default action (sh):	MOUSE: Press or click MENU on the executable glyph and select Open from the directory pane menu.
	— or —
	Select an executable, and then select Open from the file menu.
	— or —
	Press SELECT on the executable glyph. Drag to the workspace and release SELECT.
	KEYBD: Press ⎡TAB⎤ to highlight an executable, and then select Open from the file menu.

Actions Performed by the Undo Command

The following table summarizes the functions of the Undo command from the Edit menu.

Previous Command	Action Performed by Undo
Copy	The copied objects are removed, including any directories that were created as a result of a previous Copy. Files that were overwritten as a result of previous Copy commands cannot be recovered.
Move	Files or directories that were moved by a previous Move command will be placed back in the original directory. New directories are created as necessary. The moved objects are removed, including any directories created as a result of a previous Move. Files that were overwritten as a result of previous Move commands cannot be recovered.
Link	Files that were linked by a previous Link command will be accessible only from the original directory. (That is, a link will be severed.)
Delete	Undo will restore previously deleted files in the same directory, creating a new directory or directories as necessary. If you exit the File Manager application just after executing a Delete command, however, Undo will not recover deleted files.
Create Directory	A directory or directories created using a previous Create Directory command will be deleted.

Drag and Drop Accelerators

The following table summarizes the accelerators provided with the drag and drop method:

Drag an object while pressing SELECT	
Drop it on...	To perform this action...
A directory glyph on the same or another File Manager window	Copy the object.
The workspace	Execute the default action for the object (i.e., Open the object). If the object is a directory, a new File Manager base window is created which shows the contents of that directory.
Another application window	Execute the action determined by the application.

7 The Terminal Emulator Application

Introduction

Overview

The Terminal Emulator application — xterm — provides emulation for the AT&T 6386 WGS (Work Group Station) system console, and the Tektronix 4014 terminal. When emulating the AT&T 6386 console, xterm honors most of the DEC ® VT102 escape sequences and also supports standard ANSI color escape sequences. You can run any application or program from a Terminal Emulator window, and can also perform any UNIX System command in the Terminal Emulator window. In addition, in Tektronix mode you can run graphical applications such as ged(1G), stat(1G), or graph(1G).

AT&T 386 and Tektronix 4014 emulations each have their own windows, so you can edit text in one and look at the graph in the other simultaneously. However, only one window at a time has active input focus. See page 5 for information about active input focus.

Tektronix provides an "overstrike" mode instead of erasing. If you type a character and backspace over it, you see a double character. This is normal Tek 4014 behavior.

 NOTE Switching between AT&T 386 and Tek window does not change TERM, LINES, and COLUMNS environmental variables. It is up to you to set these appropriately when you move from one window into the other.

Since the Terminal Emulator application is managed by the OPEN LOOK Interface, many OPEN LOOK features are present. To understand this chapter, you should be familiar with the information on OPEN LOOK Interface functions presented in Chapters 2, 3, and 4. The section "Using the OPEN LOOK Interface," in Chapter 2 muppliep procedures for accessing the Terminal Emulator window and running applications from it.

For additional details about the Terminal Emulator application, refer to the xterm manual page in Appendix A. For the escape sequences supported in xterm, refer to Appendix B.

Organization of the Chapter

The contents of this chapter are arranged as follows:

- Accessing the Terminal Emulator Application. Includes how to start the Terminal Emulator application.

- Using the Terminal Emulator Application. Explains how to use the Terminal Emulator menus and property windows to change features and attributes of xterm.

- Mouseless Operations. Describes key sequences used for mouseless operations that should not be used in a shell running under xterm.

Accessing the Terminal Emulator Application

Create a Terminal Emulator window with the following procedure:

MOUSE:

1. Access the Workspace menu by pressing or clicking MENU on the workspace area. See the section "Operating on Menus" in Chapter 4 for details on menu access.

2. Select Programs from the Workspace menu.

3. Select Xterm from the Programs submenu.

KEYBD:

1. Press (CTRL) (w) to display the Workspace menu.

   The Programs option is highlighted.

2. Press (→) to display the submenu.

3. Type (t).

The Terminal Emulator window is shown in Figure 7-1.

Figure 7-1: The Terminal Emulator Application Window

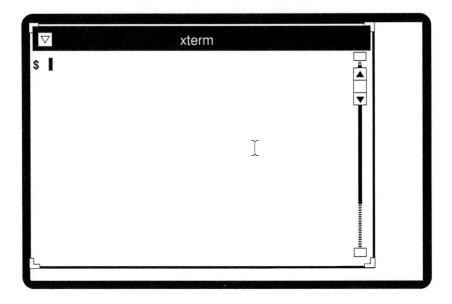

Creating Additional Terminal Emulator Windows

You can create any number of Terminal Emulator windows for as many applications as you wish to run. Simply repeat the above procedure for each window.

Automatic Login to the Terminal Emulator Window

If you want the Terminal Emulator window to appear automatically upon typing olinit, instead of accessing it from the Workspace menu, you can customize the .olinitrc file. To do this, edit .olinitrc in your home directory with the editor of your choice. Add the line xterm & to the file.

The Terminal Emulator Application Active Input Area

A Terminal Emulator window must be given active input focus in order for you to type UNIX System commands at the UNIX System prompt ($). Active input focus is indicated in the Terminal Emulator application by the solid text cursor and the highlighted header. The solid cursor and highlighted header are shown in Figure 7-1.

If the cursor is hollow, click SELECT in the pane or header, or press (**TAB**) until you attain active input focus. If you are moving back and forth from one Terminal Emulator window to another, click SELECT in the pane or header of the window when you move to it. When you create a new Terminal Emulator window, the new window will have active input focus until you select another window.

Do not confuse the text cursor with the pointer. The text cursor appears only in a window and is controlled by the keyboard, indicating where the next text you type will appear.

Running an Application in a Terminal Emulator Window

To run an application in an xterm window:

1. Position the mouse pointer anywhere in the pane and click the SELECT button to give the window active input focus.

2. At the UNIX System prompt, type the command that will initiate the application you want to run. Press (⏎).

Using the Terminal Emulator Application

The Terminal Emulator application provides the following three menus with which to perform window functions:

- Window menu. The Window menu provides the same functions as described in the subsection "Window Menu" under "Menus" in Chapter 3.

- xterm menus. AT&T 6386 and Tektronix 4014 emulations have similar but separate menus, both of which provide commands specific to the Terminal Emulator application. Both xterm menus have a Properties item, which is used to access one of the two Terminal Emulator property windows. Depending on which mode you are in, the property window controls settings specific to the Terminal Emulator application, so you can configure the application to your specifications.

The xterm Menus

The xterm menus contain commands which perform individual functions for the Terminal Emulator application. You can select any menu entries to activate the indicated functions.

To access the xterm menu, you:

MOUSE:

1. Position the pointer in the Terminal Emulator window pane.

2. Press or click MENU.

KEYBD:

1. Press ⌈TAB⌋ to establish input focus in the Terminal Emulator window pane.

2. Press ⌈F4⌋ or ⌈CTRL⌋ ⌈m⌋ to display the xterm menu.

See the subsection "Choosing from Menus" in the "Menu Operations" section of Chapter 4 for details on menu access.

AT&T 6386 Console Emulation xterm Menu

Figure 7-2 shows the xterm menu for the AT&T 6386 console emulation.

Figure 7-2: The AT&T 6386 Mode xterm **Menu**

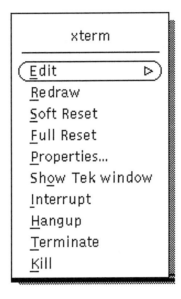

The following explains each item on the AT&T 6386 mode xterm menu.

- Edit. Calls up the edit menu. See the following section, "Edit Menu" for information.

- Redraw. Redraws the Terminal Emulator window.

- Soft Reset. Resets the scrolling region.

- Full Reset. Clears the screen and resets the terminal modes back to the defaults. Resets the tabs to their default positions.

- Properties. Invokes the xterm properties window, described on page 15.

- Show Tek Window. This item enables you to move back and forth between the AT&T 6386 window and the Tektronix window. If you select this, the Tektronix window is displayed with active input focus. The AT&T 6386 window will remain on the screen, and the menu item will toggle to read, "Hide Tek Window." If you select Hide Tek Window, the Tektronix window disappears from the screen and the AT&T 6386 window becomes active. The label will then change back to read, "Show Tek Window."

- Interrupt. Sends an interrupt signal to stop the application running in the window, including any associated UNIX System processes.

- Hangup. Sends a hangup signal to stop the application running in the window, including any associated UNIX System processes, and exits the Terminal Emulator window.

- Terminate. Sends a terminate signal to the application running in the window, including any associated UNIX System processes.

- Kill. Sends a kill signal to the application running in the window, including any associated UNIX System processes. Exits the Terminal Emulator window.

The Edit Menu

When you select Edit from the AT&T 6386 mode Xterm menu, you invoke the Edit menu. This gives you menu access to the Cut, Copy, and Paste functions. Cut, Copy, and Paste manipulate text in the VT window. You can access these functions using either a mouse or keyboard. (Editing is not possible in the Tek window.) It is not possible to perform text selection functions in the Xterm window using the keyboard; these procedures can be performed using a mouse only.

The edit menu also supplies the Send item, which combines Copy and Paste in one motion. Figure 7-3 shows the Edit menu.

Figure 7-3: Edit Menu

Send
Paste
Copy
Cut(X)

Before selecting one of the items from the Edit menu, select a portion of text by pressing the SELECT mouse button and sweeping across the characters you wish to copy. The text will be highlighted as you sweep across.

NOTE	You cannot select text with the "sweeping" procedure if you are using a keyboard.

Then use the menu functions as follows:

■ Send. Copies the highlighted text and places it at the cursor location.

■ Paste. The text in the clipboard (either copied or cut) is inserted on the Terminal Emulator pane at the location of the cursor.

■ Copy. Copies the highlighted text to the clipboard in preparation to paste it at another location. The selected text remains in place but the highlighting ceases once you select Copy.

■ Cut. Removes a single character or any number of lines from the pane to a clipboard in preparation for pasting it at another location. The highlighted text disappears from its original location.

NOTE While Copy and Cut are available only for the AT&T 6386 window, Paste can be performed on the Tek window.

Using Send, Paste, and Copy between Applications

You can Send, Paste, and Copy from another application into the Terminal Emulator application. For example, you can highlight a portion of text in another application window and select Send from the Edit menu in your Terminal Emulator window. The highlighted text will appear at the cursor in the Terminal Emulator window. Because you cannot change another application, you are unable to Cut from another application, or Paste or Send into another application.

However, if you have two Terminal Emulator windows on the screen, you can use the Send, Paste, and Copy functions on both menus. Highlight a block of text on one window and select Copy to put it in a clipboard. When you return to the other Terminal Emulator window, selecting Paste from that edit menu will paste it at the cursor.

Keyboard Equivalents of Cut, Copy, and Paste

The Cut, Copy, and Paste functions are also available from the keyboard. All keyboard equivalents described below are the OPEN LOOK-provided defaults. If you want to change these keys, see the section, "Keyboard Functions Workspace Property Window" in Chapter 5.

- Cut. Select a portion of text by pressing SELECT and sweeping across the characters you wish to cut. This can be a single character, or any number of lines. The text will highlight as you sweep across. Press (**SHIFT**) (**DELETE**) to cut the text from the pane and move it to a clipboard.

- Copy. Select a portion of text by pressing SELECT and sweeping across the characters you wish to copy. This can be a single character, or any number of lines. The text will highlight as you sweep across. Press (**CTRL**) (**INSERT**) to copy the text from the pane into a clipboard. The text will remain on the pane, no longer highlighted.

- Paste. Press (**SHIFT**) (**INSERT**) to put the text from the clipboard to the pane starting at the cursor position.

NOTE You cannot perform the text "sweeping" procedure if you are using a keyboard.

Keys Defined by a Non-OPEN LOOK Application

When you use a text editor or any non-OPEN LOOK application in the Terminal Emulator window, remember that some of the key combinations defined by that editor may already be in use for the Cut, Copy, and Paste functions. The OPEN LOOK-defined key mapping listed above will override a non-OPEN LOOK application's key mapping. For example, if you are using an editor that defines (CTRL) (INSERT) as quitting the application, when you press that combination of keys, you will get the OPEN LOOK-defined default, which is "Copy."

You can solve this conflict by mapping your OPEN LOOK functions to different keys. Compare the OPEN LOOK defaults with any keystroke functions used by the application in question, and change the key combinations on the Keyboard Functions Workspace Property window so that the OPEN LOOK-defined keys are different from those of your application. See the section, "Keyboard Functions Workspace Property Window," in Chapter 5 for information on changing these keys.

Tektronix Mode xterm Menu

The following explains each item on the Tektronix Mode xterm menu:

- PAGE. Clears the screen, resets the line style to solid lines and the font to large, sets the graphics position to HOME, moves the cursor home, and terminates the GIN (Graphics INput) mode.

- RESET. Same as PAGE, except it does not clear the screen.

- COPY. Saves the contents of the Tektronix window into a file. The name of the file will be COPY*yyMMddhhmm*, where *yy, MM, dd, hh*, and *mm* are the year, month, day, hour, and minute the copy was performed. The file is created in the directory from which the Terminal Emulator application is started, or from the home directory for an xterm login.

The other seven buttons function in the same way as the buttons on the AT&T 6386 console mode xterm menu.

Figure 7-4 shows the xterm menu for the Tektronix mode.

Figure 7-4: The Tektronix Mode xterm **Menu**

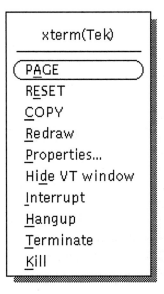

Terminal Emulator Property Windows

You control properties and features with the Terminal Emulator property windows. Each xterm menu invokes a different property window. To access these windows, select Properties from the xterm menu of the mode you are in.

Both Terminal Emulator property windows have the following features:

- Title: xterm

- Pushpin

- Apply button. Press Apply to keep the features you select.

- Reset button. Press Reset to return everything back to its original state.

The AT&T 6386 Mode Property Window

You change features of xterm by clicking SELECT on the check boxes in the AT&T 6386 mode property window. Clicking SELECT on an unchecked box will put a check in the box and select the feature. Clicking SELECT on a checked box will remove the check and therefore de-select the feature.

If you are using a keyboard, press (TAB) to move to the list of check boxes; then use the (↑) (↓) (→) and (←) keys to select the desired check box. Pressing (spacebar) on an unchecked box will put a check in the box; pressing (spacebar) on a checked box will remove the check, and, therefore, the feature.

The following explains the items on the Terminal Emulator property window.

- Visual Bell. Determines whether the Terminal Emulator application will feature a visible bell (i.e., flashing) or an audible bell when a (CTRL) (g) is received. The default is audible bell.

- Jump Scroll. Specifies whether or not pointer jumping during scrolling should be used. The default is jump scroll is used.

- Auto Wraparound. Specifies whether or not auto-wraparound should be enabled. The default is enabled.

- Auto Linefeed. When enabled, a new line, vertical tab, and new page cause a carriage return. The default is no auto linefeed.

- Application Pad. Enables the keypad. The default is `not enabled`.

- Margin Bell. Specifies whether or not the margin bell should be activated when the user types near the right margin. The default is `not activated`.

- Curses Resize. Specifies that `xterm` should allow its window to be resized while running the curses applications (e.g., `vi`). Some curses applications do not detect window resizing. If not selected, `xterm` will prevent the window from being resized. The default is `no curses resize`.

- Logging. Specifies whether or not the terminal session should be logged. You can log from only one window at a time. The default is `not logged`.

- Reverse Video. Specifies whether or not foreground and background colors should be reversed. The default is `no reverse video`.

- Reverse Wraparound. Specifies whether or not reverse-wraparound should be enabled. The default is `not enabled`.

- Application Cursor. Enables the arrow keys. The default is `not enabled`.

- Scrollbar. Specifies whether or not the scrollbar should be displayed. The default is `scrollbar is displayed`.

- Secure Keyboard. This item is not yet activated as part of the Terminal Emulator application.

Figure 7-5 shows the AT&T 6386 mode property window.

Figure 7-5: The AT&T 6386 Mode Property Window

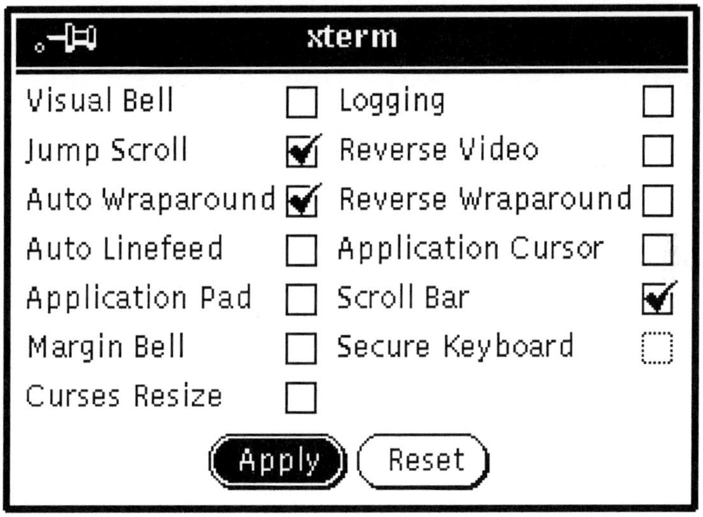

The Tektronix Mode Property Window

You select one of four font sizes on the Tektronix property window by clicking SELECT on one of the exclusive settings:

- Large Characters. 35 rows x 74 columns. This is the default font.

- Medium Characters. 38 rows x 81 columns.

- Small Characters. 58 rows x 121 columns.

- Tiny Characters. 64 rows x 133 columns.

Figure 7-6: The Tektronix Mode Property Window

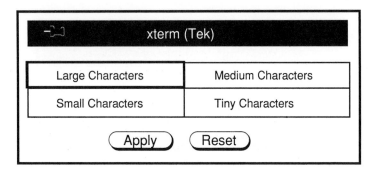

Mouseless Operations

The key sequences shown in this section are used for mouseless operations but cannot be entered to a shell running under xterm. If it is necessary to send any of these key sequences to the shell, you must re-bind the appropriate function to a different key sequence.

For VT100 Mode:

Function	Default Binding	xterm Use
Scroll up	<Prior>	Scroll xterm text up
Down	<Next>	Scroll xterm text down
Up	<CTRL><Prior>	Scroll xterm up one page
Down	<CTRL><Next>	Scroll xterm down one page
Top	<Alt><Prior>	Scroll xterm text to top of buffer
Bottom	<Alt><Next>	Scroll xterm text to bottom of buffer
Vertical Scrollbar Menu	<CTRL>r	Bring up Scrollbar Menu
Menu	<CTRL>m	Bring up xterm VT100 menu
Cut	<Shift><Delete>	Cut Text
Copy	<CTRL><Insert>	Copy Text
Paste	<Shift><Insert>	Paste Text

For Tek Mode:

Function	Default Binding	xterm Use
Menu	<CTRL>m	Bring up xterm Tek menu

8 The Administration Manager Application

Introduction

The Administration Manager application enables the system administrator to administer network connections to both the StarLAN Network and Ethernet. The Administration Manager application is invoked from the Utilities submenu of the workspace menu. Only the `root` login can use the Administration Manager application, unless the system administrator at your site has given you access to this application by specifically granting you write permissions on the relevant files. On UNIX System V Release 3.2, these files are `/usr/X/lib/Xconnections` for Outgoing Remote Displays and on `/etc/X0.hosts` for Accepted Remote Hosts. On UNIX System V Release 4, the only relevant file is `/etc/X0.hosts` since outgoing network connections are administered through Network Administration under `sysadm`.

The buttons on the Network Administration command windows are active or inactive (dimmed) depending on the permissions of the files. You can use the Network Administration application if the buttons are in an active state. If the buttons are in an inactive state, that means you are denied access to this application, although you can still read the files in the scrolling lists.

This chapter describes how to access the Administration Manager application from the workspace menu, and administer network connections from the Administration Manager windows. This chapter also gives a brief overview of how to administer network connections on systems running UNIX Systen V Release 4.

Using the Administration Manager

The Administration Manager application is available through the Utilities sub-menu on the workspace menu. To access the Administration Manager application, perform the following steps:

MOUSE:

1. Access the workspace menu by pressing or clicking MENU on the workspace area. See the section "Operating on Menus" in Chapter 4 for details on menu access.

2. Select Utilities from the workspace menu.

3. Select Network Administration from the Utilities submenu.

KEYBD:

1. Press ⌐CTRL⌐ ⌐w⌐ to display the workspace menu.

2. Type ⌐u⌐ to access the Utilities menu.

3. Type ⌐n⌐ to access the Network Administration submenu.

The Network Administration submenu provides two choices for UNIX System V Release 3.2 systems or one choice for UNIX System V Release 4 systems:

- Accepted Remote Hosts. Accepted remote host connections refers to the remote host from which your machine is authorized to accept connections.

- Outgoing Remote Displays. Outgoing remote display connections are displays on remote hosts to which a client can request a connection (UNIX System V Release 3.2 only.)

Accepted Remote Hosts

Select "Accepted Remote Hosts" from the Network Administration submenu to invoke a pop-up command window. By entering a remote host name in the Host Name field, the OPEN LOOK server on this machine will be permitted to accept network connections from clients running on the specified remote host. This will take effect the next time you start the OPEN LOOK Interface. Figure 8-1 shows the Accepted Remote Hosts pop-up command window.

Figure 8-1: Administration Manager Accepted Remote Hosts

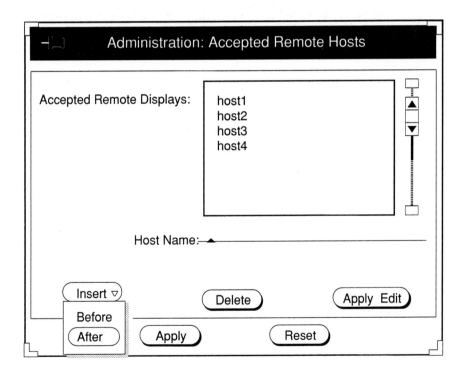

The Accepted Remote Hosts window contains the following elements:

- Title: Administration: Accepted Remote Hosts

- An editable scrolling list labeled "Accepted Remote Hosts."

- A text field labeled "Host Name:"

- Apply button. Select this button to apply your edits and exit the window.

- Reset button. Select this button to reset the scrolling list to the state before the last Apply operation.

- Insert menu button. The Insert menu button submenu has two buttons which enable you to insert new data into the scrolling list:

  □ Before. Select this button to insert a remote host name before the current item.

  □ After. Select this button to insert a remote host name after the current item.

- Delete button. Select this button to delete the current item.

- Apply Edit button. Select this button once you make changes with Insert, or add or change text in a text field.

Accepted Remote Hosts Edit Operation

To edit the scrolling list on the Accepted Remote Hosts window, do the following:

MOUSE:

1. Click SELECT on an item in the scrolling list to select it as the current item. The current item is the item that you operate on. You will do one of the following to the current item, depending on which buttons you select:

   - Insert information before the current item

   - Insert information after the current item

■ Delete the current item

■ Edit the current item

2. Insert, delete, or edit by selecting the appropriate button:

■ Insert. Select the Insert menu button for a submenu with Before and After buttons. The Insert operation accepts the name of a remote host, which you type in the text field labeled Host Name directly below the scrolling list. The input is placed either before or after the current item.

Select Before to insert a remote host name before the current item. A space opens up before the current item and the name you type into the text field moves into that space.

Select After to insert a remote host name after the current item. A space opens up after the current item and the name you type into the text field moves into that space.

■ Delete. Select Delete to delete the current item. You can type new information into the text field.

3. Once you have made your changes with Insert or Delete, select Apply Edit to set the changes.

4. Select Apply to apply all edits and exit the window, or select Reset to cancel your changes and return the scrolling list to its previous state.

KEYBD:

1. Press ⌈**TAB**⌋ to move input focus to the scrolling list.

2. Press ⌈↑⌋ or ⌈↓⌋ to select an item on the list.

3. Press ⌈**spacebar**⌋ to select the item.

4. Insert, edit, or delete by selecting the appropriate button. Descriptions of each button are provided above in the "MOUSE" section.

5. Once you have made your changes, press ⌈**TAB**⌋ until Apply Edit is selected.

6. Press (**spacebar**) to set the changes.

7. Press (**TAB**) until Apply is selected and then press (**spacebar**) to make the changes effective. If you want to cancel your changes and return the scrolling list to its previous state, press (**TAB**) until Reset is selected; then press (**spacebar**).

Outgoing Remote Displays

This section is only relevant on systems running UNIX System V Release 3.2, for UNIX System V Release 4 systems, see the section titled "Network Administration on UNIX System V Release 4" in this chapter.

Select "Outgoing Remote Displays" from the Network Administration submenu to invoke a pop-up command window. By entering a display name, host name, and network type in the text fields Display Name, Host Name, and Netspec, OPEN LOOK clients on this machine will be permitted to connect to the specified display on the specified remote host using the specified network type.

Valid Netspec types are "starlan" and "it." For example, to connect to host machine "my6386" over the network "starlan," the display name could be "my6386-s."

The Outgoing Remote Display window contains the following elements:

- Title: Administration: Outgoing Remote Displays

- An editable scrolling list labeled "Outgoing Remote Displays."

- Three text fields. Text fields are labeled Display Name, Host Name, and Netspec, to correspond to information displayed in the scrolling list.

- Apply button. Select this button to apply your edits and exit the window.

- Reset button. Select this button to reset the scrolling list to the state before the last Apply operation.

- Insert menu button. The Insert menu button submenu has two buttons which enable you to insert new data into the scrolling list:

  □ Before. Select this button to insert a remote host name before the current item.

  □ After. Select this button to insert a remote host name after the current item.

- Delete button. Select this button to delete the current item.

- Apply Edit button. Select this button once you make changes with Insert, or add or change text in a text field.

Figure 8-2 shows the Outgoing Remote Display pop-up command window.

Figure 8-2: Administration Manager Outgoing Remote Displays

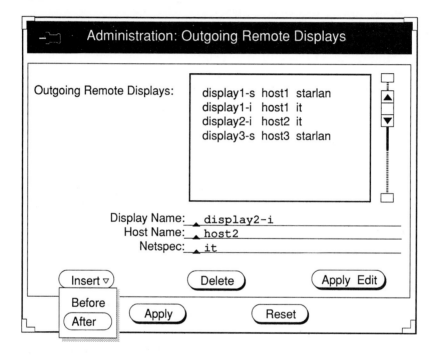

Outgoing Remote Display Edit Operation

To edit the scrolling list on the Outgoing Remote Display window, perform the following procedure:

MOUSE:

1. Click SELECT on an item in the scrolling list to select it as the current item. The current item is the item that you operate on. You will do one of the following to the current item, depending on which buttons you select:

   ■ Insert information before the current item

   ■ Insert information after the current item

   ■ Delete the current item

   ■ Edit the current item

   When you select the current item, the three text fields automatically fill in the information as shown in the scrolling list. For example, Figure 8-2 shows a window in which the entry

   ```
   display1-i  host2  it
   ```

   was selected. That information is displayed in the text fields below the scrolling list.

2. Edit the scrolling list by selecting the appropriate button of the following:

   1. Insert. Select the Insert menu button for a submenu with Before and After buttons. Type the new information in the text fields directly below the scrolling list. The input is placed either before or after the current item.

      Select Before to insert information before the current item. A space opens up before the current item and the name you type into the text field moves into that space.

      Select After to insert information after the current item. A space opens up after the current item and the name you type into the text field moves into that space.

2. Delete. Select Delete to delete the current item. You can type new information into the text fields to replace the data you deleted.

3. Once you have made your changes with Insert or Delete, select Apply Edit to set the changes.

4. Select Apply to apply all edits and exit the window, or select Reset to cancel your changes and return the scrolling list to its previous state.

KEYBD:

1. Press ⎡**TAB**⎤ until the scrolling list becomes highlighted.

2. Press ⎡↑⎤ or ⎡↓⎤ to select an item in the scrolling list.

3. Press ⎡**spacebar**⎤.

4. Edit the scrolling list by selecting the appropriate button; the buttons are described above in the MOUSE section.

5. Once you have made your changes with Insert or Delete, press ⎡**TAB**⎤ to select Apply Edit. Press ⎡**spacebar**⎤.

6. Press ⎡**TAB**⎤ until Apply becomes selected; press ⎡**spacebar**⎤ to apply all edits. If you want to cancel your changes and return the scrolling list to its previous state, press ⎡**TAB**⎤ until Reset becomes selected; then press ⎡**spacebar**⎤.

Network Administration on UNIX System V Release 4

On UNIX System V Release 4, the Administration Manager Application is not used to administer the network; it is done through sysadm. On UNIX System V Release 3.2 systems, the XWIN server uses the directory /usr/X/lib/net to determine the available networks when listening for connections. On SVR4 systems, the XWIN server uses the SHELL variable NETPATH instead. NETPATH can be set as follows:

```
NETPATH="net1:net2:...:netN"; export NETPATH
```

where net1, net2, ..., netN are network identifiers (NID). Each NID must match the first column of an entry in the network configuration table /etc/netconfig. If NETPATH is not set, the server will attempt to listen to all networks listed in /etc/netconfig.

On SVR3.2 systems, XWIN clients wishing to establish connections with remote servers use the table /usr/X/lib/Xconnections to determine available networks. On SVR4 systems, XWIN clients use the SHELL variable NETPATH for that purpose. Clients will try to connect to a remote server via the networks represented by the NID's listed in the NETPATH variable. The networks will be tried one after the other, in the order listed, until a connection succeeds. If NETPATH is not set, all the networks listed in /etc/netconfig will be tried. If a connection cannot be established with the remote server, the Xlib call XOpenDisplay() will fail.

For each network, there are two files that need to be updated: hosts and services. For TCP/IP, these two files resides in /etc, for STARLAN they reside in /etc/net/starlan.

On the client side, the hosts file must have a line containing the address of the remote host running the server. On the server side, if you want the server to listen for connections over a particular network, an entry for the server's host is required in the hosts file for that network. Each entry in a hosts file must have the following format:

```
host-name     host-address
```

Where the structure of host-address is network dependent. For example, the file /etc/hosts will have entries like this:

```
foo           186.23.45.137
```

while /etc/net/starlan/hosts will have entries like this:

```
foo           foo-uname
```

The services files describe what port the server will be listening on for connections. There should one entry for each display. If your machine has more than one display, there will be multiple entries in each services file. For TCP/IP, the file /etc/services should have the following entry for Display 0:

```
xserver0     6000/tcp
```

For STARLAN, the file `/etc/net/starlan/services` should have the following entry for `Display 0`:

    xserver0   0

 NOTE For more complete information on Administering the Network on SVR4 systems, see the SVR4 manual "Network User's and Administrator's Guide."

Running SVR3.2 clients on an SVR4 System

There is a new daemon for name to address translation on SVR4 called `xntad` (X name to address daemon.) This daemon is intended only for clients that were compiled and linked with the X static shared library on an SVR3.2 machine. This daemon will use the name-to-address translation library in SVR4 to do the translation rather than forking a nameserver. The `xntad` can only be used in conjunction with the upgraded shared library, Xlib Version 2.0 or higher. The functionality provided by `/usr/X/lib/Xconnections` will be replaced by the SHELL variable `NETPATH` described above. The new daemon, `xntad`, is executed automatically at boot time on SVR4 systems. If you will not be using any clients that where compiled and linked on an SVR3.2 system, you may not want the daemon to execute automatically at boot time. If you do not want the daemon to execute at boot time, delete the following files:

    /etc/init.d/xwin
    /etc/rc2.d/K95xwin
    /etc/rc3.d/S95xwin

9 The Print Screen Application

Introduction

Overview

The Print Screen application gives you a menu selection with the ability to cap-ture, display, and print all or portions of a window or screen. This application combines the features of the commonly used XWIN commands xpr, xwd, xwud, and the UNIX System command lp.

To capture an image (window, area of a screen, or the entire screen) on the Print Screen pane, select the Window, Area, or Screen item from the Capture Image menu button. The application will momentarily disappear and return with the desired image in its pane.

Once the image is captured in the pane, you can save it by selecting the Save As item from the File menu button. Once a file is saved, you can use the Open item to redisplay it at any time.

To print the contents of the Print Screen pane, select Print Contents from the Print menu button. To print an already saved file, select Print File from the Print menu button.

If you are using OPEN LOOK with a keyboard, you should be aware that, although you can access the Print Screen menu items using mnemonics, you may NOT be able to complete all the functions unless you are using a mouse. For example, the Capture Image, Print Window and Print Area functions are NOT available if you are using OPEN LOOK with a keyboard. Therefore, it is recommended that you do not attempt to access the Print Screen functions from the keyboard.

 NOTE The correct output format and print command for your site must be set before you can print anything. See your system administrator for information on changing the print commands on the Print Screen properties window.

To capture an image and direct it automatically to a printer without displaying it in the Print Screen pane, select Window, Area, or Screen from the Print menu button.

To change properties for the default file name, the image formatting settings, and print settings, select the Properties window button.

When you select one of the print functions, xpr and lp will be executed, with options specified from the saved settings of your most recent "Apply" or "Set Defaults" invocation. Any subsequent errors will appear in the file $HOME/.oliniterr, and any messages from xpr and lp will appear in the file $HOME/.olinitout.

Accessing the Print Screen Application

The Print Screen application is available through the Utilities submenu on the workspace menu. To access the Print Screen application, perform the following steps:

MOUSE:

1. Access the workspace menu by pressing or clicking MENU on the workspace area. See the section "Operating on Menus" in Chapter 4 for details on menu access.

2. Select Utilities from the workspace menu.

3. Select the Print Screen window button from the Utilities submenu.

When you select Print Screen from the workspace menu, the following window appears:

Figure 9-1: The Print Screen Base Window

When the Print Screen base window first appears, it consists only of a border with resize corners, a title, and control area containing four buttons. The first time it captures an image, a pane appears beneath the control area and the image is captured within the pane. The Print Screen window expands its borders to accommodate the pane, which enlarges to display the image. If the image is too large to fit within the pane, vertical and/or horizontal scrollbars appear. You can further expand the pane's size manually by using the resize corners.

Using the Print Screen Application

The Print Screen window control area contains the following buttons:

- File (menu button). Select this menu to save or display file contents.

- Print (menu button). Select this menu to print objects from the screen without writing them to a file or showing them inside the pane.

- Capture Image (menu button). Select this menu to capture and display objects from the screen.

- Properties (window button). Select this property window to customize the defaults of the Print Screen application.

NOTE The text fields in the Print Screen application do not interpret UNIX System file name substitutions or shell variables.

Figure 9-2: The Print Screen Menus

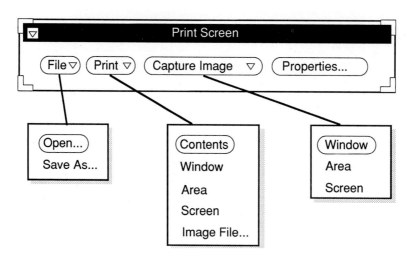

The File Menu Button

The File menu button is the first button on the Print Screen control panel. From this menu button you access the File menu, which gives you the choices of the Open and Save As items.

Figure 9-3: The File Menu

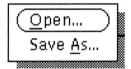

Open

Open displays an image which was previously captured in a file using Save As (see page 6) or the xwd command. Perform the following steps:

1. Select Open from the File menu by clicking SELECT on Open, or by pressing ⎡o⎤.

2. When the Open command window appears, type into the text field the name, including full or relative path, of the file you wish to display.

   The Print Screen application checks to see that the file can be opened. If the file does not exist or you mistyped the name or path, a message Cannot open file is displayed in the footer.

   The file's image content is displayed in the Print Screen window. The Print Screen window resizes itself for the contents displayed.

3. You can manually enlarge it still further with the resize corners.

   If at any time the image shown in the window is larger than the Print Screen window, scrollbars will appear in the Print Screen window to enable you to scroll the contents.

NOTE

When using Window or Area from the Print or Capture Image menus:

Wait until all applications have refreshed themselves before selecting a window or area to be captured.

Sometimes Print Screen and Capture Screen might not allow all applications enough time to refresh themselves before the screen is captured. If this is the case, use Print Window or Capture Window instead; wait for everything to refresh, then select the background (which is the whole screen).

Save As

Save As enables you to save the image displayed in the Print Screen window into a specified file. Perform the following steps:

1. Display an image in the Print Screen window, using the Capture Image menu (see page 9).

2. Using the buttons in the control area above the image, select the file menu. Select Save As from the file menu by clicking SELECT on Save As, or by presing (a).

3. When the Save As command window appears, type a file name into the text field. This will name the image currently appearing in the Print Screen window.

   The Print Screen application checks to see that the file can be created. If not, a message Cannot create file is displayed in the footer.

   The image displayed in the Print Screen window is then created as the named file. The Save As window and the File menu you use to get this file will not appear as part of the image.

The Print Menu Button

The Print menu button is the second button on the Print Screen control panel. From this menu button you access the print menu, which gives you the following item choices:

- Contents
- Window
- Area
- Screen
- Image File

Figure 9-4: The Print Menu

Contents

The Contents selection prints the contents of the Print Screen pane.

Window

Click SELECT on Window or press ⓦ to select this item. The pointer will change appearance, shown in Figure 9-5, with text that reads, Select Window.

Figure 9-5: Select Window Pointer

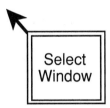

Position the cursor on the window you wish to print. Click SELECT to send the image to the printer.

 NOTE When Window, Area, or Screen is selected from the print menu or the capture image menu, the system beeps once when the process begins and twice when it has successfully finished.

Area

Follow these steps to dump and print a specific area of the screen.

1. Click SELECT on Area or press ⓐ to dump and print a specific area of the screen.

2. When the pointer changes to Select Area, press SELECT.

   A bounding box (an elastic outline) appears, which you can drag to surround the area you want to capture.

3. Release SELECT when the bounding box is the size you want. The image is then sent to the printer.

Screen

Click SELECT on Screen, or press ⓢ to print the entire screen in one step.

Image File

Click SELECT on Image File, or press ⓘ to print a previously dumped image file. When you select Image File, a command window appears into which you enter the file name of the image you wish to print.

The Print Screen application checks to see that the file can be printed. If not, a message is displayed in the footer.

If the file name is valid, the file will be sent to the printer.

The Capture Image Menu Button

The capture image menu button is the third button on the Print Screen control panel. The capture image menu gives you the following item choices:

- Window
- Area
- Screen

Capture Image captures everything within the selected area: for example, if the window you are capturing has other windows partly or completely covering it, those windows will also appear in the image. To capture one and only one object in the image, you must dismiss any other windows or move the selected window to the front of the screen.

Figure 9-6: The Capture Image Menu

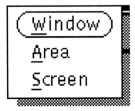

Window

This item enables you to capture and display a window in the Print Screen window. The pointer will change to a pointer with text that reads, "Select Window."

1. Click SELECT and the Print Screen application will capture the contents of the topmost window on which the cursor is positioned.

The image is then displayed in the Print Screen window.

NOTE If a second window is currently on top of the window you want to capture, bring your chosen window to the front of the screen before capturing it.

Area

Click SELECT on Area or press ⓐ in order to capture an area of the screen and display it in the Print Screen window.

1. When the pointer changes to Select Area, press SELECT.

The Print Screen base window will temporarily disappear so you have an entire screen from which to select. A bounding box appears.

2. Hold SELECT on a point of the outline and drag to surround the area you want to capture.

3. Release SELECT when the bounding box is the size you want.

The Print Screen base window returns, with the area you selected captured in its pane.

Screen

Click SELECT on this item or press ⓢ to capture the screen and display it in the Print Screen window.

Figure 9-7 shows the Print Screen window with the image of the entire screen captured. In this illustration, the original screen contained a Terminal Emulator window in the upper left of the workspace with the xclock application in a window in front of the Terminal Emulator window. The user invoked a Print Screen window (which appeared in the lower right) and selected Screen from the Capture Image menu. The Screen command captured the entire screen image of workspace, Terminal Emulator window, and clock, but the screen image is too big to fit in the pane. Vertical and horizontal scrollbars are on the Print Screen window to enable the image to scroll to view the entire screen.

Figure 9-7: Capture Image Screen Command

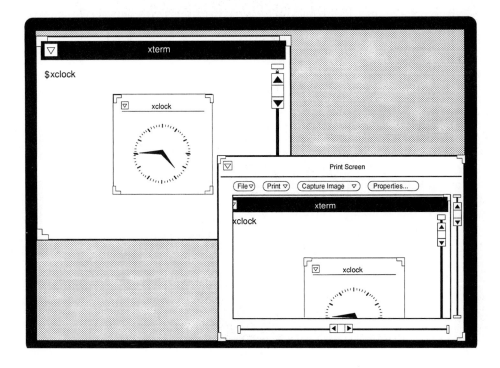

Print Screen Property Window

The Properties window button is the fourth button on the Print Screen control panel. Click SELECT on this button, or press $\boxed{\text{p}}$ to bring up a property window, as shown in Figure 9-8.

Figure 9-8: The Print Screen Property Window

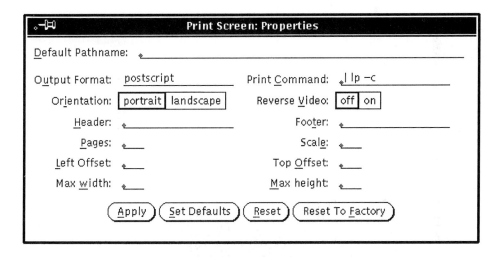

Use this property window to change default options. You can customize settings for the following attributes:

- Default pathname. This field is the file name supplied to the three pop-up command windows — Open, Save As, and Print. Your home directory will appear in this field unless you change it. This field cannot be blank.

- Output format. Enter the "−d" option, for device type, into this text field to specify the format mode used to print the window image. This is usually determined by the system administrator, and should not be changed by the novice user. This field cannot be blank.

- Print command. This text field enables you to set the `lp` command and its options. This field must be set in order for you to be able to print. Consult your system administrator for help with the `lp` command that manages the printer at your site. This field cannot be blank.

- Orientation. This item gives you a choice of two settings to determine which direction the data will print on the page. "Portrait" is upright, and "landscape" is horizontal. Default is portrait.

- Reverse video. This allows you to set reverse video, which causes the image to be printed intensity inverted. The default is off.

- Header. This lets you specify a title above the printed image.

- Footer. This lets you specify a title below the printed image.

- Pages. This specifies how many pages the printed image will be split into.

- Scale. This specifies the factor to which the printed image is scaled. Default is the largest scale that still allows the full image to be printed on a page. The suggested value is 3 for PostScript printers. Scale refers to the magnification of the image relative to its size on the screen. For example "Scale 2" means the printed picture will be twice the size of the screen image.

- Left offset. This changes the left margin. The margin is measured in inches: for example 1.5 inches. We suggest using the default and leaving the field blank.

- Top offset. This changes the top starting point of the image. The margin is measured in inches: for example 1.5 inches. We suggest using the default and leaving the field blank.

- Max width. This changes the maximum width. The margin is measured in inches: for example 1.5 inches. We suggest using the default and leaving the field blank.

- Max height. This changes the maximum height. The margin is measured in inches: for example 1.5 inches. We suggest using the default and leaving the field blank.

- Apply. Select this button to incorporate your final changes and exit. Settings take effect on the next printing.

- Set Defaults. Select this button to permanently store your applied settings to be used in subsequent Print Screen base windows. If you apply settings using this window, and select the Set Defaults button, then any other Print Screen base windows you create subsequent to this will incorporate the settings you apply here.

- Reset. Select this button to return the properties to the previously applied settings.

- Reset to Factory. Select this button to return the properties to the system default settings.

| NOTE | If you desire to use PostScript format, we recommend you type and use "ps" (dithering rendering mode) or "postscript" (grayscale rendering mode) on the Print Screen property window "Output format" field

For PostScript format, a scale of 3 (the "Scale" field in the property window) is recommended for standard size paper.

Do not execute the print command in the background (for example, do not place an ampersand (&) at the end of the property window "Print command" field).

olprintscreen might not recognize saved dumped files previously captured from different resolution colormap screens. You can use xwud to display those files (and then use olprintscreen to recapture them once they are displayed).

10 Troubleshooting

Troubleshooting

The tables in this chapter contain solutions to problems you may encounter with OPEN LOOK.

Getting Started

If this happens...	Do this...
My OPEN LOOK environment is black and white instead of color.	If you have a color monitor, you have to set the colors yourself from the Color workspace property window. Refer to the section "Color Workspace Property Window" in Chapter 5 for information on setting colors for the Window Manager and Workspace Manager applications.
My mouse buttons do not work as described in the *User's Guide*.	The illustration in the *User's Guide* shows a right-handed mouse. It is possible that a previous user changed the settings of the buttons to accommodate a left-handed user. Refer to the section "Mouse Modifiers Workspace Property Window" in Chapter 5 for information on setting the mouse buttons to suit your preference.
	If your (NUMLOCK) or (CAPSLOCK) key has been activated, the mouse buttons will not work with the Window Manager application, although the mouse pointer will continue to move and the mouse buttons may work with other applications. To avoid this problem, do not activate the (NUMLOCK) or (CAPSLOCK) keys.
Mnemonics do not work as described in the *User's Guide*.	If your (CAPSLOCK) key has been activated, mnemonics and accelerators may not work as described. When using the keyboard, take care not to press the (CAPSLOCK) key unless instructed to do so. Mnemonics are entered in lowercase, unless otherwise specified.

If this happens...	Do this...
I type `olinit` and get my prompt back but nothing happens.	Sometimes it takes a few seconds for the OPEN LOOK GUI software to startup. However, if nothing is happening after 5 or 10 seconds, you can type `ps -ef` at the UNIX system prompt and look for the `X:0`, `olinit`, `olwsm`, and `olwm` processes.
	If none of these are running, make sure you are in you home directory and type `cat .oliniterr` at the UNIX System prompt. Error messages will be found in this file that could help diagnose the problem. See the "Installation and System Administration" section of this chapter.
When I place the pointer on an object, nothing happens or an object other than the one I intended is affected.	The "hot spot" of the pointer must be on the object before you can operate on it. On the basic pointer, the hot spot is the tip of the arrow. When you want to manipulate a small button or letter of text, the tip of the arrow must be exactly on that object.
	The hot spot of the Terminal Emulator pointer is the center of the vertical bar. To manipulate a scrollbar, for example, the center of the vertical bar must be exactly on the part of the scrollbar you are trying to manipulate.
	The hot spot of the drag and drop pointer, as seen in the File Manager application, is the center of the outline. This kind of pointer is used to drag a selected object from one area to another. A rectangular outline attaches itself to the basic pointer and surrounds the object it is dragging.
When I left my computer, the screen went blank.	The OPEN LOOK Interface has a screen saver that blanks the screen after a period of keyboard and mouse inactivity. To restore it, move the mouse slightly or press a key on the keyboard.

If this happens...	Do this...
I do not know how to get on-line help.	Try pressing the [f1] function key on the keyboard. If that doesn't work, it is because a previous user has changed the default help key setting. Access the Keyboard Functions workspace property window from the Properties item on the workspace menu, to see what key is mapped to help. Refer to the section "Keyboard Functions Workspace Property Window" in Chapter 5 for information on changing keyboard equivalents. If this does not work, make sure your [NUMLOCK] or [CAPSLOCK] key is not depressed.

Windows and Menus

If this happens...	Do this...
I can't resize a window as small as I would like to.	There is a minimum window size determined by the application. You might consider closing the window into an icon.
When I click MENU in order to choose from a menu in stay-up mode, the menu disappears before I can do anything.	Large menus might not come up in stay-up mode if you click too fast. Click firmly and slowly enough to release the MENU button after the menu starts to appear on the screen, but not so slowly that it interprets your motion as a press rather than a click.
My window borders and header disappeared, and I can't access the Window menu.	You may have inadvertently caused the Window Manager to stop functioning. Do the following: Press ⟨**ALT**⟩ and ⟨**SysRq**⟩ simultaneously and then press ⟨**h**⟩. This returns you to your original UNIX environment. Type `olwm&` at the UNIX System prompt and press ⟨↵⟩. This restarts the Window Manager. Press ⟨**ALT**⟩ and ⟨**SysRq**⟩ simultaneously and then press ⟨**n**⟩. This returns you to the OPEN LOOK Interface environment.
Frozen Window: I can't enter any input at the UNIX System prompt on the Terminal Emulator window.	You must give your window active input focus. Position the pointer in the pane or header of the window and click SELECT.

If this happens...	Do this...
I clicked SELECT or pressed ⌐spacebar⌐ and the window is still frozen.	Press this sequence of keys: ⌐←⌐ ⌐CTRL⌐ ⌐z⌐ ⌐←⌐
I have tried all of the above and the window remains frozen.	Do the following: 1. Press ⌐ALT⌐ and ⌐SysRq⌐ simultaneously and then press ⌐h⌐. This returns you to your original UNIX environment. 2. Type ps -ef at the UNIX System prompt. This gives you the process number of the server (called X or X:0). 3. Type kill -2 <process_number>. This signals the server to terminate. 4. Press ⌐ALT⌐ and ⌐SysRq⌐ simultaneously. Then press ⌐p⌐. This returns briefly to the server and allows it to exit gracefully.

The Workspace Manager Application

If this happens...	Do this...
I pinned the Workspace menu and later pressed MENU again to call up a second Workspace menu. However, the one I pinned is no longer where I left it.	You can have only one Workspace menu at a time. If you invoke the Workspace menu, pin it, and then access an application, the new window might cover up the pinned Workspace menu, making it appear as if the Workspace menu has disappeared. When you press MENU on the workspace again, the existing Workspace menu comes to the front of the screen.
I changed the settings in a Workspace property window, but I don't see any evidence of that change.	You must click SELECT on the Apply button to save any changes made to a property window. If you are using a keyboard, make sure the Apply button has active input focus, then press ⎵spacebar⎵.

The File Manager Application

If this happens...	Do this...
While in the File Manager application, I selected the File menu button to access the file menu. But the Open, Copy, Move, Link, and Print buttons on the file menu are dimmed and I can't select them.	Those buttons are not activated until you select an object from the directory pane. Using either the mouse or the keyboard, select a directory, file, or executable, and then access the file menu. All of the buttons will be available once you select an object.

If this happens...	Do this...
The File Manager print command is not printing my file.	You may be trying to print a shell file with execute permission. Try removing the execute permission via a properties pop-up window and access the print command from the file menu. You can also create a Terminal Emulator window and type `lp -c filename`
I created a file using the Create File button on the file menu, but I can't see the new file listed on the directory pane.	Although creating a directory results in an immediate update, the File Manager application waits until the next update before changing the display for a newly created file.

Installation and System Administration

If this happens...	Do this...
I tried to add a user with the `oladduser` command and it didn't work.	It is possible that the files `.olsetup`, into your home directory during the process. Sample files exist in /usr/X/adm and you can copy them from there into your home directory. Perform the following steps: 1. Make sure .oladduser exists in /usr/X/adm and run /usr/X/adm/oladduser *<login>* again. If this still doesn't work, try the following: 2. Type `cd /usr/X/adm` at the UNIX System prompt. 3. Type

If this happens...	Do this...

	`cp .olinitrc` *<yourhomedirectory>*
	`cp .Xdefaults` *<yourhomedirectory>*
	`cp .olsetup` *<yourhomedirectory>*
	
	If you get messages that any or all of the above files do not exist in this directory, reinstall the End User System package and try `oladduser` again.
	
	4. Return to your home directory and edit your `.profile` file with the editor of your choice. Add the following line to the end of your `.profile` (all on one line):
	
	   `.  $HOME/.olsetup <Tab>`
	   `#@ Do not edit this line@`
	
	Remember: only the system administrator can add other users. Using `oladduser` you can only add yourself.

I am responsible for installing the OPEN LOOK Interface system, but I am not sure which other software packages and versions are already installed.	On SVR 3.2.1 and 3.2.2 only type `displaypkg` at the UNIX System prompt and press ⏎. On SVR 4.0 systems, type `pkginfo` and press ⏎. The information you need will appear on the screen.
The following warning message appears in the `.oliniterr` file in your home directory: "`Could not open default font fixed.`"	You have installed the OPEN LOOK Interface with a non-AT&T server, which does not have the OPEN LOOK Interface fonts. The uncompiled fonts are located in `/usr/x/fonts/bdf/Xol`. They must be compiled with your server's font compiler, and installed in `/usr/X/lib/fonts`.

If this happens...	Do this...
I tried to invoke an application while specifying a font and got a core dump.	If specifying a font from either the .Xdefaults file or on the command line, make sure it is a valid font and is spelled correctly.
I'm having abnormal occurrences ever since I changed some values in my .Xdefaults file.	Use this file with caution, particularly when setting values for core resources. These values affect all widgets. In particular, avoid adding data to set new values for *borderWidth and *measure.
I can't access the OPEN LOOK Interface.	It is possible that the DISPLAY variable has not been set in your environment. To correct this, be sure to run oladduser before olinit. Then log out and log in again or type $HOME/.olsetup.
The following warning message appears in my oliniterr file in my home directory: "cannot open /dev/mouse"	The OPEN LOOK GUI software requires the installation of a mouse and mouse driver. If the mouse driver was improperly installed, this message may appear.

A   Appendix A: Supported Applications

NAME

oladduser - add an OPEN LOOK user.

SYNOPSIS

oladduser

/usr/X/adm/oladduser [-s] [*user*]

oladduser resides in /usr/X/adm. Since the PATH variable does not normally include that path, you can either specify the full pathname, as shown above, or you can add /usr/X/adm to your PATH variable.

DESCRIPTION

The oladduser command adds a new OPEN LOOK user by creating the file .olsetup in the user's home directory and adding the line

. $HOME/.olsetup<TAB>#!@ Do not edit this line !@

to the end of the user's .profile. The user is specified by login name using either the optional argument *user* or by entering the login name on standard input when prompted for it.

In addition, oladduser will create the file .Xdefaults with default settings, and the .olinitrc file with the following lines:

olwm &

olfm &

If the user already exists, .Xdefaults will be moved to .Xdefaults.old and the other files will be overwritten. If write permissions are not granted on any of these files, oladduser will write an error message on standard error stating so, and exit.

The oladduser procedure automatically sets and exports the XWINFONTPATH environment variable which ensures that the OPEN LOOK GUI fonts are found by the XWIN server. If the oladduser procedure is not executed when OPEN LOOK is installed, and the user has not explicitly set the $XWINFONTPATH environment variable, the system-wide default will be used.

OPTIONS

-s   This option causes the user to be set up to invoke OPEN LOOK at each login.

FILES

$HOME/.olsetup
$HOME/.Xdefaults
$HOME/.profile
$HOME/.olinitrc

SEE ALSO

olremuser(1), olsetvar(1)

NAME

olinit - initialize the OPEN LOOK Graphical User Interface

SYNOPSIS

olinit [[*client*] *options*] [-- [*server*] [*display*] *options*]

DESCRIPTION

The olinit program is similar to the original X Window System xinit program, but is described here in detail to outline the difference. Aside from naming conventions, the major difference is that the default primary client is the OPEN LOOK workspace manager instead of xterm.

The olinit program is used to start the X Window System server, a primary client program (the OPEN LOOK workspace manager), and (optionally through an .olinitrc file) secondary clients (for example, window manager or xterm). When the primary client exits, olinit will kill the X server and then terminate. If the X server exits, olinit will kill the primary client and the secondary clients and then terminate.

Unless otherwise specified on the command line, olinit assumes that there are programs called X and olwsm in the current search path. It starts the server on display 0 and then runs olwsm.

An alternate primary client and/or server may be specified on the command line. The desired client program and its arguments should be given as the first command line arguments to olinit. To specify a particular server command line, append a double dash (--) to the olinit command line (after any client and arguments) followed by the desired server command.

A relative or full pathname must be provided for the primary client program and the server program. Otherwise, they are treated as arguments to be appended to their respective startup lines. This makes it possible to add arguments (for example, foreground and background colors) without having to retype the whole command line.

If an explicit server name is not given and the first argument following the double dash (--) is a digit, the olinit program will use that number as the display number instead of zero. All remaining arguments are appended to the server command line.

olinit also creates files called .oliniterr and .olinitout and places them in the user's home directory. All errors and warnings are put in the .oliniterr file. Output to stdout is written out to the .olinitout file.

An .olinitrc file can be used to start secondary clients if olwsm is the primary client. Since it is the responsibility of olwsm to execute the .olinitrc file, the contents of .olinitrc will be ignored if an application other than olwsm is the primary client for olinit. olwsm looks for this file in the user's home directory. The format of this file is typically:

```
client_a &
client_b &
```

It is recommended that a `sleep` command be inserted after `olwm&` in `.olinitrc` if additional clients are added, so that the Window Manager will be started before the other secondary clients. For example,

```
olwm&
sleep 5
xeyes&
```

FILES

```
$HOME/.olinitrc
$HOME/.oliniterr
$HOME/.olinitout
```

NOTE

`olinit` can only be used for starting the server and clients on the same machine. Using `olinit` with remote servers is not supported in this release.

`olinit` can be used to change the screen resolution to one of three different resolutions with the following command:

```
olinit -- -lines [600] [480] [400]
```

NAME

olpixmap - pixmap editor

SYNOPSIS

olpixmap [-options...] [*filename*]

DESCRIPTION

The olpixmap editor is a software product that allows users (primarily software developers) to create and edit pixmaps that may be used by other X Window System applications. olpixmap is intended for use mainly by software developers to create pixmaps for use in their applications, but can also be useful to end users in creating custom background pixmaps for their root window (see xsetroot(1), which has been modified to accept pixmap files).

The olpixmap editor is an independent, self-contained component of the OPEN LOOK product. It is meant as a complement to the bitmap program provided by MIT as part of the X Window System.

As an interactive application, olpixmap reacts to user input (usually by manipulating the mouse) to set pixels in a pixmap to specific colors. Users have available to them convenient primitive operations for drawing simple closed shapes and lines, as well as filling arbitrarily shaped areas with a specified color.

The pixmap editor does not support mouseless operations within the pixmap grid. The only mouseless operations supported are navigation between controls and windows, and mnemonics and accelerators.

The output of olpixmap is a small C code fragment. By #include'ing such a program fragment into an application, the user can easily declare the size and content of icons, window backgrounds, and other pixmaps that an application creates to deal with the X Window System.

The olpixmap editor writes pixmaps in the XPM (X PixMap) file format. The XPM format is a convention for storing pixmaps on disk in a portable (ASCII), device-independent (no depth or color limitations), #include'able format, similar to MIT's standard X11 bitmap file format.

Applications wanting to read or write this format will need to link in two source files to provide this support. These files (xpm.c and xpm.h) are installed by olpixmap for such use, and can be found (typically) in /usr/X/lib/tutorial/XPM on SVR3.2 machines and in /usr/lib/X11/tutorial/XPM on SVR4.0 machines.

DEFINITIONS, ACRONYMS, AND ABBREVIATIONS

Pixmap   A pixmap is a three dimensional array of bits. A pixmap is normally thought of as a two dimensional array of pixels, where each pixel can be a value from 0 to 2^N-1, where N is the depth (z axis) of the pixmap. A pixmap can also be thought of as a stack of N bitmaps.

Pixel   A pixel is an N-bit value (at a single point), where N is the number of bit planes (for example, the depth of) used in a particular pixmap.

Depth	The depth of a pixmap is the number of bits per pixel it has.
Bitmap	A bitmap is a pixmap of depth 1.
Press	A press is the down transition of a mouse button or key.
Release	A release is the up transition of a mouse button or key.
Click	A click is a button press followed by a button release with no intervening mouse motion (any mouse damping factor is taken into account).
Dragging	Dragging refers to a button press followed by some amount of mouse motion (greater than the mouse damping factor), terminated by a button release.

Mouse Damping Factor
> The mouse damping factor is the amount the mouse is allowed to actually move in between a button press and a button release while still considering the button press/release combination to be a click.

Sweeping	Sweeping is mouse motion with a mouse button down; similar to dragging.
Canvas	The canvas is the area in which the pixmap is actually manipulated.

OVERVIEW:
STARTUP BEHAVIOR

olpixmap comes up with a base window plus a pinned popup window. The base window consists of a canvas pane displaying a magnified image of a pixmap, in which each pixel is shown as a large square (as if on a piece of graph paper), and a button control area. The popup shows the pixmap at its actual size, with a single-pixel wide box outlining the portion of the pixmap being magnified.

When olpixmap starts, it first tries to read the specified file. If the file already exists, it creates a canvas pane containing a grid of the appropriate dimensions. If the file does not exist, olpixmap will create a pane for a pixmap of the default size, and the pixmap will start out empty.

SELECT, ADJUST, and MENU

SELECT is used to start working with (for example, start the drawing process of) the current object. For the case of a single pixel, clicking SELECT sets the chosen pixel to the current color, while dragging SELECT sets all pixels dragged through. In the case of lines or line segments, pressing SELECT sets the initial endpoint; releasing SELECT sets the terminal endpoint. For other objects (for example, oval or rectangle), pressing SELECT sets the center or corner of the bounding rectangle. Subsequent dragging of SELECT changes the size of the bounding rectangle. The object is drawn the appropriate size upon release of SELECT.

ADJUST currently has no function.

MENU is used to bring up a menu.

CONTROL LAYOUT

olpixmap has a canvas pane to display the magnified pixmap located to the left of a control panel. The control panel has buttons and menu buttons labeled File, View, Edit, Draw, Palette, and Properties. The functionality associated with each button is listed under the appropriate heading.

File

Selecting File pops up a window with a text field and buttons for opening and saving a pixmap.

Open reads in a fresh pixmap file.

Browse allows interactive traversal of the file system for selection of a pixmap file to open.

Save writes out the current pixmap file.

Detailed explanations of the open and save operations can be found in the sections labeled "Reading Files In", "Browsing", and "Writing Files Out".

View

Show Pixmap (the default button) allows the user to pop up a window containing the actual size pixmap on which the user is working. The pixmap in the popup window is updated in real time with any operations the user performs. (This button is used to re-popup this window if the one from start-up is unpinned.)

The Zoom In button is the second control. It allows the user to zoom in to a higher magnification level on the current pixmap. Successive zoom-ins are supported.

The Zoom Out button is the inverse operation of the Zoom In button. Selecting Zoom Out returns the pixmap to the previous level of magnification.

Edit

The Fill button enables the user to fill a portion of the pixmap to the current color.

Clear provides a quick way to clear out a specified rectangular area of the pixmap.

The Copy button enables the user to copy selected areas of the pixmap.

Move works in a similar fashion to Copy.

The Roll function horizontally or vertically rotates the pixmap, with wrapping around at the edges.

Further details of the controls in the Edit menu can be found in the appropriately labeled sections that follow.

Draw

The Draw menu consists of an exclusive setting from which the user can choose the current drawing function.

Pixels enables the user to set arbitrary pixels.

Lines allows the user to draw lines by selecting two endpoints.

Segments is similar to Lines, letting the user draw connected line segments. Each subsequent endpoint specified after the first two draws a connecting line from the previous one.

Ovals enables the user to draw arbitrary ovals by sweeping the bounding rectangle on the pixmap.

Circles is a constrained case of the general Ovals function.

Rectangles lets the user draw arbitrary rectangles by sweeping the rectangle on the pixmap.

Squares is a constrained case of the general Rectangles function. Further details of the controls in the Draw menu can be found in the appropriately labeled sections that follow.

Palette   Pressing the Palette menu button displays a submenu showing the different drawing colors available. The current drawing color can be changed by choosing a new entry from this menu.

Properties   The Properties button pops up a property window that allows the user to choose the current line width, line style, grid appearance, and pixmap dimensions.

Further details of the controls in the Properties property window can be found in the appropriately labeled sections that follow.

COMMANDS

Reading Files In

Choosing Open from the File window initiates a read from the file named in the text field. Any previous work is discarded and the new pixmap file is read in, with the canvas being resized as necessary. Any error messages related to reading the specified file will be displayed in the window footer. `olpixmap` supports reading of standard X11 bitmap format files.

Browsing   The Browse window is a pop-up window with its pushpin initially unpinned. Choosing Browse from the File window will pop up a File Manager window from which the user can traverse through the file system and potentially choose a pixmap file to open. Double-click SELECT on the icon of the desired pixmap file in order to load it into the pixmap editor. The browse operation can be cancelled if desired via a File Manager submenu.

Alternatively, the user can take advantage of the "drag and drop" feature to open pixmap files shown in already-existing File Manager windows. Using SELECT, drag the desired file from an independent File Manager window, and drop it onto the magnification pane of `olpixmap`. The file will then be opened as usual.

Writing Files Out

Choosing Save from the File window writes the current pixmap to the file named in the text field (which by default is the last one opened). If there is an existing file by that name, it will be renamed with an appended tilda character. Any error messages related to writing the specified file will be displayed in the window footer.

Show Pixmap

Selecting the Show Pixmap button pops up a window that contains a actual size representation of the pixmap currently being edited. If the window is already popped up, then it will be raised to the front. This pixmap is updated as the user works on the canvas.

Magnifying   Magnification is accomplished by the use of the Zoom In and Zoom Out buttons. The Zoom In button increases the level of magnification for the canvas pane (scrollbars are added if not already present). The pixel representations are sized accordingly. Any number of Zoom In operations may be performed up to the point of having a single pixel fill the viewport. Subsequent Zoom In requests are ignored. The Zoom In operations are stacked; the Zoom Out button returns the canvas to the previous magnification value. If the user has not zoomed in, no operation is performed.

Fill Area   When Fill is chosen, the user is directed to select a point within the area that s/he desires to fill. All pixels in that area that are of the same color as the one chosen will be filled to be the current color. Thus, the fill stops at the boundaries of where the color is not the same as that of the chosen point.

Clear Area   Choosing Clear prompts the user to sweep out a rectangular area to clear to the background color.

Copy Area   When Copy is chosen, the user is directed to sweep an area of the canvas by dragging SELECT, indicating the area to be copied. When SELECT is released, the user is instructed to specify, by pressing SELECT, the location where the upper left corner of the copied area is to begin. When SELECT is released, the area is copied.

Move Area   When Move is chosen, the user is directed to sweep an area of the canvas by dragging SELECT indicating the area to be moved. When SELECT is released, the user is instructed to specify, by pressing SELECT, the location where the upper left corner of the swept area is to be moved. When SELECT is released, the area is moved. Any pixel "exposed" by the move operation will be set to the background color.

Roll   This function will horizontally and/or vertically rotate the pixmap, with wrapping around at the edges. The user makes this happen by choosing a point within the pixmap to make the new upper-left corner of the pixmap. This point will first be rolled horizontally to the left edge of the pixmap, with all pixel data to its left wrapping around to the right edge of the pixmap, and then the point is rolled vertically to the top edge of the pixmap, with all pixel data above wrapping around to the bottom edge of the pixmap. This function is useful when creating a pixmap that needs to join with itself when tiled.

Drawing Raw Pixels
             The user may set individual pixels by selecting the Pixels item under the Draw menu button. When the user is drawing raw pixels, SELECT sets the pixel pointed to by the mouse to the current color.

Drawing Lines
             To draw a collection of lines, the user would first select the Lines button. The user would then be prompted to select the initial endpoint by pressing SELECT over some pixel. A rubber band line

would appear anchored to the selected pixel, tracking the pointer. When the user would release the button, the terminal endpoint is selected and the line is drawn using the current color, line width, and line style.

Drawing Connected Segments

Drawing connected line segments follows a similar interface to drawing lines. The user selects the initial endpoint of the first segment by pressing SELECT. A rubber band line tracks the pointer until the user releases the button, causing the line to be drawn in the current color using the current line width, and line style. To draw another segment, the user again presses SELECT. However, for this and all subsequent segments, the initial endpoint is anchored at the terminal endpoint of the previously drawn segment. When SELECT is pressed, a rubber band line appears, anchored at the terminal endpoint of the previous segment, tracking the pointer. When SELECT is released, the next segment is drawn.

Drawing Ovals

Selecting Ovals prompts the user to sweep the bounding box for the oval. When the user presses SELECT, a rubber banding rectangle is drawn, centered about the pixel over which SELECT was pressed. The appropriate corner (lower right, if the user pulls down and to the right; upper left, if the user pulls up and to the left, etc.) tracks the pointer until the user releases SELECT. An oval is then drawn to the size specified by the bounding rectangle, using the current color, line width, and line style.

Drawing Circles

Circles are drawn in an identical manner to ovals. The constraint of a square bounding box is automatically imposed.

Drawing Rectangles

Selecting Rectangles prompts the user to sweep the bounding box for the rectangle. When the user presses SELECT, a rubber banding rectangle is drawn, centered about the pixel over which SELECT was pressed. The appropriate corner tracks the pointer until the user releases SELECT. A rectangle is then drawn to the size specified by the rubber banding rectangle, using the current color, line width, and line style.

Drawing Squares

Squares are drawn in an identical manner to rectangles. The constraint of a square bounding box is automatically imposed.

Changing the Current Color

The color used for drawing operations may be changed using the Palette submenu. This menu displays a box for each of the available colors in the colormap. The menu can be pinned for rapid access.

PROPERTIES

The Properties property sheet allows the user to set the values of various parameters pertaining to the operation of olpixmap. New values may be chosen by manipulating the controls; these values are then put into effect by clicking SELECT on the "Apply" button. The user may choose the "Reset" button at any time to return the controls to the values currently in effect.

Line Width   The Line Width slider allows the user to change the width of objects drawn (lines, ovals, rectangles, etc.). The slider displays the current line width (zero by default). This value may be changed by the user to any integer value.

Line Style   The Line Style item allows the user to select the line type. Line type is selected by choosing one of the two exclusive settings, "Solid" (the default) or "Dashed."

Grid Appearance

The Grid item is an exclusive setting that controls whether the canvas grid will be shown; selecting "Off" inhibits the display of the grid.

Pixmap Dimensions

The Pixmap Width and Height fields show the dimensions of the pixmap currently being edited. Either or both of these values may be dynamically changed by typing a valid integer value into the appropriate fields (and subsequently selecting the "Apply" button). Any error messages will be displayed in the window footer.

The pixmap is resized to the size requested by the user, with any pixel values being copied into the new pixmap. If the new pixmap is larger than the old pixmap, the old pixmap will be copied intact, starting at (0,0), with the remainder of the new pixmap being unset. If the new pixmap is smaller, the old pixmap is copied starting at (0,0) and clipped by the boundary of the new pixmap. The magnification pane is sized appropriately.

FILE FORMAT

olpixmap reads and writes files in the following format (XPM), which is suitable for #include'ing in a C program:

```
#define name_format 1
#define name_width 16
#define name_height 16
#define name_ncolors 4
#define name_chars_per_pixel 1
static char * name_colors[] = {
" " , "#FFFFFFFFFFFF",
"." , "SkyBlue",
"X" , "#000000",
"o" , "ForestGreen"
} ;
static char * name_pixels[] = {
```

```
"X..X        X",
" X..X        X",
" X..X       X ",
"  X..X     X ",
"  X..X    X  ",
"  X..X   X  ",
"   X..X  X  ",
"   X.. X   ",
"   XX X    ",
"   X ooX    ",
"   X XooX   ",
"   X XooX   ",
"   X XooX   ",
"  X    XooX ",
" X        XooX ",
" X        XooX"
};
```

The *name* portion of the shown variables will be derived from the name of the file specified either on the original command line or in the File window by deleting the directory path (all characters up to and including the last '/', if one is present), and deleting the extension (the first '.', if one is present, and all characters beyond it).

For example, invoking `olpixmap` with the filename
`/usr/X/include/X11/pixmaps/cross.xpm` on SVR3.2 systems or
`/usr/include/X11/pixmaps/cross.xpm` on SVR4 systems will produce a file with variable names *cross_width*, *cross_height*, *cross_ncolors*, *cross_chars_per_pixel*, *cross_colors*, and *cross_pixels*.

It's easy to define a pixmap in an X program by simply #include'ing a pixmap file and referring to its variables. For instance, to use a pixmap defined in the file `cross.xpm`, one simply writes:

```
#include "cross.xpm"
```

```
Pixmap cross = XCreatePixmapFromData(DISPLAY, DRAWABLE, COLORMAP,
                          cross_width, cross_height, DEPTH,
                          cross_ncolors, cross_chars_per_pixel,
                          cross_colors, cross_pixels);
```

Colors will be allocated from the supplied colormap as necessary, and the pixmap cross (which will be created with the specified depth) could then be used like any normal X pixmap.

An X program can also read a pixmap file at runtime by using the function `XReadPixmapFile()`.

SEE ALSO
        bitmap(1)

NAME

olprintscreen - OPEN LOOK® Print Screen application

SYNOPSIS

olprintscreen &

DESCRIPTION

olprintscreen is the OPEN LOOK Print Screen client.

The Print Screen application gives you a menu selection with the ability to display, capture, and print all or portions of a window or screen. You cannot use the keyboard to operate on the Capture Image, Print Window, or Print Area functions.

If executed manually (on the shell command line) in a window, olprintscreen will output printing messages (from lp) to that window's standout out (stdout).

EXAMPLES

olprintscreen &

SEE ALSO

OPENLOOK(1)

COPYRIGHT

See OPENLOOK(1) for a full statement of rights and permissions.

NAME

   olremuser - remove an OPEN LOOK user.

SYNOPSIS

   olremuser [*user*]

DESCRIPTION

   The olremuser program removes an existing OPEN LOOK user by removing the
   files .olsetup, .olinitrc, and .Xdefaults from the user's home directory
   and removing the line that matches

   . $HOME/.olsetup<TAB>#!@ Do not edit this line !@

   from the user's .profile. If write permissions to remove or change the specified
   files are not granted in the user's home directory, olremuser will write an error
   message on standard error stating so and exit. If the user was not an OPEN
   LOOK user, this command will fall through.

FILES

   $HOME/.olsetup
   $HOME/.olinitrc
   $HOME/.Xdefaults
   $HOME/.profile

SEE ALSO

   oladduser(1)

NAME

.olsetup - executes *olinit* from a user's $HOME/.profile.

SYNOPSIS

$HOME/.olsetup

DESCRIPTION

.olsetup is a front end shell script that invokes olinit from a user's
$HOME/.profile. It will set the value of the shell variable OLINVOKE. If this
variable is set to **yes**, it will execute the command

/usr/X/bin/olinit /usr/X/bin/olwsm -- -xnetaccess $XNETACCESS

where the variable XNETACCESS contains the current value of network access
(values are either **on** or **off**). There is one copy of the script $HOME/.olsetup for
each OPEN LOOK user. .olsetup will also set the XWINFONTPATH variable
to include the OPEN LOOK fonts.

FILES

$HOME/.profile

SEE ALSO

oladduser(1), olinit(1)

NAME
      olsetvar - sets a shell variable to a value in the user's $HOME/.olsetup file.

SYNOPSIS
      olsetvar - variable value [user]

DESCRIPTION
      The olsetvar program edits the file ~user/.olsetup (~user refers to the home
directory of the user user) to add a shell assignment statement with the variable
variable to the value *value*. The variable is exported as well so that programs that
shell .olsetup will have these new variables set in their respective environments.
If a user is not specified through user, $HOME is the home directory used. This
command is used by the OPEN LOOK workspace manager to assign the variable
OLINVOKE a value and it is used by the command oladduser to set up other
variables.

      If the name of the login ID is not the same as the $HOME variable, the user
should invoke olsetvar with the login ID on the command line.

      olsetvar will ensure that no duplicate entries of variable assignments are made.
If a value already exists for the specified variable, olsetvar will reset this value
to the new value. olsetvar will write an error message on standard error and
exit if the ~user/.olsetup does not exist, if the *user* does not exist, or if write
permissions are not granted on the user's ~user/.olsetup file.

EXAMPLES
      olsetvar OLINVOKE yes usera

      olsetvar PATH '$PATH:/usr/X/bin'

FILES
      $HOME/.olsetup

SEE ALSO
      oladduser(1), olunsetvar(1)

NAME

olunsetvar - removes a shell variable assignment entry from the user's $HOME

SYNOPSIS

olunsetvar - variable [user]

DESCRIPTION

The olunsetvar program edits the file ~user/.olsetup (˜user refers to the home directory of the user **user**) to remove the shell assignment statement, if it exists, containing the variable *variable*. If a user is not specified using *user*, $HOME is used as the home directory.

FILES

$HOME/.olsetup

SEE ALSO

olsetvar(1), olsetup(1)

NAME

olwm - OPEN LOOK™ Window Manager

SYNOPSIS

olwm [*display*]

DESCRIPTION

olwm is the AT&T window manager embodying the look and feel of OPEN LOOK. It allows the user to create, move, resize, raise, lower, iconify, and delete windows.

olwm takes one optional command line argument: the X display name. Additionally, olwm will look in the .Xdefaults file in the user's home directory for some user-specifiable parameters.

The following is a list of these parameters along with acceptable values.

Foreground: color of title displayed in header, color of menu button, pushpin

Background: color of window header

NAME

resize - utility to set TERMCAP and terminal settings to current window size

SYNOPSIS

resize [-u] [−s [*row col*]]

DESCRIPTION

resize prints a shell command for setting the TERM and TERMCAP environment variables to indiciate the current size of xterm window from which the command is run. For this output to take effect, resize must either be evaluated as part of the command line (usually done with a shell alias or function) or else redirected to a file which can then be read in. From the C shell (usually known as /bin/csh), the following alias could be defined in the user's .cshrc:

```
%  alias rs 'set noglob; `eval resize`'
```

After resizing the window, the user would type:

```
%  rs
```

Users of versions of the Bourne shell (usually known as /bin/sh) that don't have command functions will need to send the output to a temporary file and the read it back in with the "." command:

```
$  resize >/tmp/out $  . /tmp/out
```

OPTIONS

The following options may be used with resize:

−u   This option indicates that Bourne shell commands should be generated even if the user's current shell isn't /bin/sh.

−c   This option indicates that C shell commands should be generated even if the user's current shell isn't /bin/csh.

−s [*rows columns*]
This option indicates that that Sun console escape sequences will be used instead of the special xterm escape code. If *rows* and *columns* are given, resize will ask the xterm to resize itself. However, the window manager may choose to disallow the change.

FILES

/etc/termcap   for the base termcap entry to modify.

/.cshrc   user's alias for the command.

SEE ALSO

csh(1), tset(1), xterm(1)

NOTES

The −u or −c must appear to the left of −s if both are specified.

There should be some global notion of display size; termcap and terminfo need to be rethought in the context of window systems. (Fixed in 4.3BSD, and Ultrix-32 1.2)

NAME

xterm – terminal emulator for X

SYNOPSIS

xterm [–*toolkitoption* ...] [–option ...]

DESCRIPTION

xterm is a terminal emulator designed specifically for use in the OPEN LOOK Interface or the XWIN Graphical Window System. It emulates the AT&T 6386 WGS system console. xterm also supports most of the DEC VT102™ escape sequences. The escape sequence ESC7 is part of xterm Tektronix mode emulation to allow applications to programmatically switch from Tektronix emulation to VT102 emulation. When running on a color console, xterm honors the ANSI standard color escape sequences. Thus, curses-based color applications can run under xterm.

Each invocation of xterm produces a separate X window, in which terminal emulation is performed. This emulation allows non-X applications to be run from within the X environment.

Although more than one X window may be displayed concurrently, only one X window may accept keyboard input at a time. The window which is currently accepting keyboard input is known as the "active" window. The active window is selected by using the SELECT pointer button.

You can use mouseless operations to access the xterm menu and to operate the scrollbar. You can also use mnemonics for all xterm menu options. However, mouseless operations will not work for text selection.

OPTIONS

xterm accepts all of the following options:

–b *positive integer*
> This option specifies the size of the inner border (the distance between the outer edge of the characters and the window border) in pixels. It can range between 3 and 40. The default is 3.

–cr *color*
> This option specifies the color to use for text cursor. The default is black.

–C
> This option allows console logging for SVR4 systems **only**. When xterm is invoked with the –C option, xterm displays all console messages written to the log driver. Messages written directly to /dev/console will not be picked up.

–e *program [arguments* ...]
> This option specifies the program (and its command line arguments) to be run in the xterm window. The default is to start the user's shell. This must be the last option on the command line.

–fb *font*
> This option specifies a font to be used when displaying bold text. There is no default.

It is the user's responsibility to select a bold font with the same height and width as the normal font. If only one of the normal or bold fonts is specified, it will be used as the normal font and the bold font will be produced by overstriking this font.

-j   This option indicates that **xterm** should use jump scrolling. The default is jump scrolling is used.

+j   This option indicates that **xterm** should not use jump scrolling.

-l   This option indicates that **xterm** should send all terminal output to a log file as well as to the screen. This option can be enabled or disabled using the Xterm property window. The default is no logging.

+l   This option indicates that **xterm** should not do logging.

-lf *filename*
           This option specifies the name of the file to which the output log described above is written. If *file* begins with a pipe symbol (|), the rest of the string is assumed to be a command to be used as the endpoint of a pipe. The default filename is "**XtermLog**.*XXXXX*" (where *XXXXX* is the process id of the parent **xterm** process) and is created in the directory from which **xterm** was started (or the user's home directory in the case of a login window). Note that logging can be done in only one window at a time.

-ls   This option indicates that the shell that is started in the **xterm** window be a login shell, i.e. the first character of argv[0] will be a dash, indicating to a shell that it should read the user's .**login** or .**profile**.

-mb   This option indicates that **xterm** should ring a margin bell when the user types near the right end of a line. This option can be turned on and off from the Xterm property window. The default is off.

+mb   This option indicates that margin bell should not be rung.

-ms *color*
           This option specifies the color to be used for the mouse pointer. The default is black.

-n *string*
           This option specifies the icon name for **xterm**'s windows. The default icon name is **xterm**.

-nb *positive integer*
           This option specifies the number of characters from the right end of a line at which the margin bell, if enabled, will ring. The default is 10.

-r   This option indicates that reverse video should be simulated by swapping the foreground and background colors. It is equivalent to **-rv**. The default is no reverse video.

-rs   This option specifies that a user can resize an xterm window while a curses-based application is running.

+rs   This option does not allow the user to resize an xterm window while a curses-based application is running.

−rw   This option indicates that reverse-wraparound should be allowed. This allows the cursor to back up from the leftmost column of one line to the rightmost column of the previous line. This option can be turned on and off from the Xterm property window. The default is off. Note that wraparound must be enabled for reverse wraparound to work.

+rw   This option indicates that reverse-wraparound should not be allowed.

−sb   This option brings Xterm up with a scrollbar.

+sb   This option brings Xterm up without a scrollbar. The default is with scrollbar.

−sl *positive integer*
     This option specifies the number of lines to save that have been scrolled off the top of the screen. The default is 64. The maximum allowed is 256.

−t   This option brings up **xterm** in Tektronix mode.

−T *string*
     This option specifies the title for **xterm**'s windows. It is equivalent to −title. The default name is **xterm.**

−vb   This option indicates that a visual bell is preferred over an audible one. Instead of ringing the terminal bell whenever a <CNTRL>-G is received, the window will be flashed. The default is audible.

+vb   This option indicates that a visual bell should not be used.

The following command line arguments are provided for compatibility reasons. They may not be supported in the next release as the X Toolkit provides standard options that accomplish the same task.

−w *positive integer*
     This option specifies the width in pixels of the border surrounding the window. It is equivalent to −bw. It can range between 1 and 40. The default width is one pixel.

     The following standard X Toolkit command line arguments are commonly used with **xterm:**

−bd *color*
     This option specifies the color to use for the border of the window. The default is "black."

−bg *color*
     This option specifies the color to use for the background of the window. The default is "white."

−bw *positive·integer*
     This option specifies the width in pixels of the border surrounding the window. It is equivalent to −w. The default width is one pixel.

-display *display*

    This option specifies the X server to contact; the default is `unix:0` and specifies the console device. See X(1).

-fg *color*

    This option specifies the color to use for displaying text. The default is "black".

-fn *font*

    This option specifies the font to be used for displaying normal text. The default font is "lucidatypewriter." An appropriate size will be chosen at startup based on screen resolution, to give a 12-point font. In all cases where there is no corresponding bold font, the regular font is used in its place. The fonts **xterm** supports are: fixed, 6x10, 8x13, 8x13bold; see /usr/X/lib/fonts/misc on SVR3.2 or /usr/lib/X11/fonts/misc on SVR4 for more fonts.

-geometry *geometry*

    This option specifies the preferred size and position of the **xterm** window in characters.

    This argument is specified as –geometry *WxH±X±Y*, with *W* = width in columnar characters and *H* = number of rows. *X* and *Y* are always measured in pixels with the upper left corner *X* pixels to the right and *Y* pixels below the upper left corner of the screen (origin (0,0)).

    The maximum **H** is 128 and maximum **W** is 200.

    Note that if the window is larger than the screen, **xterm** will automatically reduce its size to the size of the screen. Also note that **olwm** may modify geometry requests if the resulting window is totally off-screen.

    "WxH" can be omitted to obtain the default application size, or "+X+Y" can be omitted to obtain the default application position (which is usually then left up to the window manager or user to choose). The X and Y values may be negative to position the window off the screen. In addition, if minus signs are used instead of plus signs (for example, WxH-X-Y), then (X,Y) represents the location of the lower right hand corner of the window relative to the lower right hand corner of the screen.

-i

    This option indicates that **xterm** should ask the Window Manager to start it as an icon rather than as the normal window.

-name *name*

    This option specifies the application name under which resources are to be obtained, rather than the default executable file name.

-rv

    This option indicates that reverse video will be affected by swapping the foreground and background colors. The default is no reverse video.

-xrm *resourcestring*

    This option specifies a resource string to be used. This is especially useful for setting resources that do not have separate command line options.

X DEFAULTS

The program understands all of the core X Toolkit resource names and classes as well as:

name (class Name)
> Specifies the application name under which resources are to be obtained, rather than the default executable file name.

"title (class Title)
> Specifies a string that will be displayed in the header of the window, if the window manager is running.

The following resources are private to xterm.

allowSendEvents (class AllowSendEvents)
> Specifies whether or not synthetic key and button events (generated using the X protocol SendEvent request) should be interpreted or discarded. The default is "false," meaning that they are discarded. Note that allowing such events creates a very large security gap.

background (class TextBackground)
> Specifies the color to use for the background of the window. The default is "white." The background will be the same color as the "Text Background" color specified on the Workspace Manager's Color Property Sheet. If you do not specify the background in the .Xdefaults file, different values for *Background* and *Text Background* will cause the xterm menus and text windows to have different background colors.

boldFont (class Font)
> Specifies the name of the bold font. There is no default.

borderColor (class BorderColor)
> Specifies the color of the border surrounding the xterm text window. The default is "black."

console (class Console)
> Allows the user to turn on the command line option (–C) for SVR4 systems only. When xterm is invoked with the –C option, xterm displays all console messages written to the log driver. Messages written directly to /dev/console will not be picked up.

cursesResize (class CursesResize)
> When "true," specifies that a user may resize the xterm window while a curses-based application is running. When "false," specifies that a user may not resize the Xterm window while a curses-based application is running. The default is "false."

font (class Font)
> Specifies the name of the normal font. The default is "lucidatypewriter." See –fn for other supported fonts and more information.

`fontColor` (class `TextFontColor`)
> This dynamic resource specifies the color to use for displaying text in the window. Setting the class name instead of the instance name is an easy way to have everything that would normally appear in the "text" color change color. The default is "black."

`geometry` (class `Geometry`)
> Specifies the preferred size and position of the VT102 window.

`iconName` (class`IconName`)
> Specifies the icon name for **xterm** window. See −n option.

`inputFocusColor` (class `Foreground`)
> This dynamic resource specifies the color to use for the text cursor. The default is "black."

`internalBorder` (class `BorderWidth`)
> Specifies the number of pixels between the characters and the window border. The default is 3.

`jumpScroll` (class `JumpScroll`)
> Specifies if jump scrolling should be used. The default is "true."

`logFile` (class `Logfile`)
> Specifies the name of the file to which a terminal session is logged. The default is "`XtermLog.XXXXX`" (where *XXXXX* is the process id of the parent **xterm** process).

`logging` (class `Logging`)
> Specifies whether or not a terminal session should be logged. The default is "false." Note that logging can be done in only one window at a time.

`logInhibit` (class `LogInhibit`)
> Specifies whether or not terminal session logging should be inhibited. The default is "false."

`loginShell` (class `LoginShell`)
> Specifies whether or not the shell to be run in the window should be started as a login shell. The default is "false."

`marginBell` (class `MarginBell`)
> Specifies whether or not the bell should be run when the user types near the right margin. The default is "false."

`nMarginBell` (class `Column`)
> Specifies the number of characters from the right margin at which the margin bell should be run, when enabled. The default is 10 characters from the end of the line.

`pointerColor` (class `Foreground`)
> Specifies the color of the pointer. The default is "black."

`reverseVideo` (class `ReverseVideo`)
> Specifies whether or not reverse video should be affected. The default is "false."

reverseWrap (class ReverseWrap)
> Specifies whether or not reverse-wraparound should be enabled. The default is "false."

saveLines (class SaveLines)
> Specifies the number of lines to save beyond the top of the screen when a scrollbar is turned on. The maximum is less than 256. The default is 64.

scrollBar (class ScrollBar)
> Specifies whether or not the scrollbar should be displayed. The default is "false."

signalInhibit (class SignalInhibit)
> Specifies whether or not the entries in the "xterm X11" menu for sending signals to xterm should be disallowed. The default is "false."

tekInhibit (class TekInhibit)
> Specifies whether or not Tektronix mode should be disallowed. The default is "false."

tekStartup (class TekStartup)
> Specifies whether or not xterm should start up in Tektronix mode. The default is "false."

visualBell (class VisualBell)
> Specifies whether or not a visible bell (for example, flashing) should be used instead of an audible bell when Control-G is received. The default is "off."

TERMINAL EMULATION

xterm VT102 emulation is fairly complete but does not support the blinking character attribute nor the double-wide and double-size character sets.

SCROLLBAR

The scrollbar represents the position and amount of text currently displayed in the window relative to the amount of text actually saved. As more text is saved (up to the maximum), the elevator moves to the bottom of the scrollbar.

Pressing the SELECT pointer button on the middle portion of the elevator and moving the mouse cursor up or down results in scrolling up or down through the scrolling region.

Clicking SELECT on the up or down arrow (at each end of the elevator) moves the visible text region up or down one line.

Pressing SELECT on the up or down arrow scrolls the visible text region one line at the time until the SELECT is released or the margin of the text buffer is reached.

Clicking SELECT on the top or bottom box of the scrollbar moves the visible region to the top or bottom of the text buffer.

Clicking SELECT in the scroll region above or below the elevator moves the visible region one page up or down.

MENUS

xterm has two menus which can be accessed by pressing or clicking the MENU button while on the Xterm window pane. The Xterm menus contain commands which perform individual xterm functions. Choosing a button to select any of the entries on the menus activates the indicated functions. Notable entries in the command sections of the menus are the Interrupt, Hangup, Terminate and Kill, which send the SIGINT, SIGHUP, SIGTERM and SIGKILL signals, respectively, to the process group of the process running under xterm (usually the shell). The Properties entry on the Xterm menu causes a property window to display. This property window sets various modes in the xterm emulation, among them auto wraparound, auto linefeed, and reverse wrap.

ENVIRONMENT

xterm sets the environment variable TERM properly for the type of display you are using, TERM=xterm on color displays and TERM=xtermm on monochrome displays. Modifying corresponding terminfo entries will produce undesirable and irrevocable damage to the X operating environment and require reinstallation of the X package. xterm also uses and sets the environment variable DISPLAY to specify which bitmap display terminal to use. The environment variable WINDOWID is set to the X window id number of the xterm window. If you run applications which use TERMCAP, use TERMCAP=`infocmp -C`; export TERMCAP whenever creating or resizing a window.

NOTES

If a user invokes the UNIX System exec command from an xterm window, it is the xterm process which will disappear. This is correct behavior but most likely not desirable. See exec SH(1) for more detail.

Applications which close stdin, stdout, and/or stderr may produce unpredictable results and should be avoided.

If the display is monochrome and options in an .Xdefaults file or on a command line specify background and foreground colors that would produce black on black or white on white, xterm provides a default of black on white.

xterm responds dynamically to changes in text foreground, text background, and input focus color; these values can be changed via the OPEN LOOK Workspcae Manager.

If the stty settings you use are not those used by xterm, you may need to import your "stty" environment to xterm; for example, interrupt, erase, and kill characters. However, caution should be used in the redefinition of these values. xterm does not inherit stty settings set prior to starting xterm.

You should not attempt to modify the terminfo entries xterm and xtermm. This will preclude the mouse from working with FMLI and require reinstallation of the AT&T XWIN Graphical Windowing System.

On the AT&T Intel-386 based product line, CONSEM can be set for better performance, but this will provide a lesser degree of console emulation support for certain ioctls (for example, CONSEM=yes; export CONSEM).

If you exec an application that creates its own window (such as MS-DOS) and then try to change the input focus to the **xterm** window which exec-ed the application, the next attempt to input to that window will cause the **xterm** window and the exec-ed process to die. This is due to the nature of exec (see **exec**(2)). The recommendation is not to exec programs like MS-DOS.

xterm may hang if you try to paste too much text at one time. It is both producer and consumer for the pty and can deadlock. Should **xterm** hang, the <RETURN><CTRL-Z><RETURN> sequence will return the prompt.

Variable-width fonts are not handled reasonably.

<CTRL-BREAK> does not work in an **xterm** window.

The **-w** option is not available for this release. Instead, use the **-bw** option for the same function.

<CTRL-G> (bell), <CTRL-L> (vertical tab), and <CTRL-k> (form feed) are not available for use on 3B2s running UNIX SVR4.0.

B Appendix B: xterm Control Sequences

xterm Control Sequences

Definitions

C A single (required) character.

P_s A single (usually optional) numeric parameter, composed of one or more digits.

P_m A multiple numeric parameter composed of any number of single numeric parameters, separated by ⎡;⎤ character(s).

P_t A text parameter composed of printable characters.

VT102 Mode

Most of these control sequences are standard VT102 control sequences. There are, however, additional ones to provide control of *xterm* dependent functions, like the scrollbar or window size.

BEL	Bell (Ctrl-G)
BS	Backspace (Ctrl-H)
TAB	Horizontal Tab (Ctrl-I)
LF	Line Feed or New Line (Ctrl-J)
VT	Vertical Tab (Ctrl-K)
FF	Form Feed or New Page (Ctrl-L)
CR	Carriage Return (Ctrl-M)
ESC # 8	DEC Screen Alignment Test (DECALN)
ESC (C	Select G0 Character Set (SCS)

                $C = $ 0 ⟶ Special Character and Line Drawing Set

                $C = $ 1 ⟶ Alternate Character ROM Standard Set

                $C = $ 2 ⟶ Alternate Character ROM Special set

                $C = $ A ⟶ United Kingdom (UK)

                $C = $ B ⟶ United States (USASCII)

ESC 7	Save Cursor (DECSC)
ESC 8	Restore Cursor (DECRC)
ESC =	Application Keypad (DECPAM)
ESC >	Normal Keypad (DECPNM)
ESC D	Index (IND)

`ESC` `E`	Next Line (NEL)
`ESC` `H`	Tab Set (HTS)
`ESC` `M`	Reverse Index (RI)
`ESC` `T` P_s `LF`	Change Window Title to P_s
`ESC` `[` P_s `@`	Insert P_s (Blank) Character(s) (default = 1) (ICH)
`ESC` `[` P_s `A`	Cursor Up P_s Times (default = 1) (CUU)
`ESC` `[` P_s `B`	Cursor Down P_s Times (default =1) (CUD)
`ESC` `[` P_s `C`	Cursor Forward P_s Times (default = 1) (CUF)
`ESC` `[` P_s `D`	Cursor Backward P_s Times (default =1) (CUB)
`ESC` `[` P_s `;` P_s `H`	Cursor Position [row;column] (default =[1,1]) (CUP)
`ESC` `[` P_s `J`	Erase in Display (ED)

$P_s = \boxed{0} \longrightarrow$ Clear Below (default)

$P_s = \boxed{1} \longrightarrow$ Clear Above

$P_s = \boxed{2} \longrightarrow$ Clear All

`ESC` `[` P_s `K`	Erase in Line (EL)

$P_s = \boxed{0} \longrightarrow$ Clear to Right (default)

$P_s = \boxed{1} \longrightarrow$ Clear to Left

$P_s = \boxed{2} \longrightarrow$ Clear All

`ESC` `[` P_s `L`	Insert P_s Line(s) (default = 1) (IL)
`ESC` `[` P_s `M`	Delete P_s Line(s) (default = 1) (DL)
`ESC` `[` P_s `P`	Delete P_s Character(s) (default = 1) (DCH)
`ESC` `[` P_s `c`	Device Attributes (DA1)
`ESC` `[` P_s `;` P_s `f`	Cursor Position [row;column] (default = [1,1]) (HVP)
`ESC` `[` P_s `g`	Tab Clear

$P_s = \boxed{0} \longrightarrow$ Clear Current Column (default)

$P_s = \boxed{3} \longrightarrow$ Clear All

`ESC` `[` P_s `h`	Mode Set (SET)

$P_s = \boxed{4} \longrightarrow$ Insert Mode (IRM)

$P_s = \boxed{2}\ \boxed{0} \longrightarrow$ Automatic Linefeed (LNM)

`ESC [ `P_s` l`	Mode Reset (RST)
	$P_s = $ `4` $\longrightarrow$ Insert Mode (IRM)
	$P_s = $ `2` `0` $\longrightarrow$ Automatic Linefeed (LNM)
`ESC [ `P_s` m`	Character Attributes (SGR)
	$P_s = $ `0` $\longrightarrow$ Normal (default)
	$P_s = $ `1` $\longrightarrow$ Blink (appears as Bold)
	$P_s = $ `4` $\longrightarrow$ Underscore
	$P_s = $ `5` $\longrightarrow$ Bold
	$P_s = $ `7` $\longrightarrow$ Inverse
`ESC [ 3`P_s` m`	Set foreground color
`ESC [ 4`P_s` m`	Set background color
	$P_s = $ `0` $\longrightarrow$ Black
	$P_s = $ `1` $\longrightarrow$ Red
	$P_s = $ `2` $\longrightarrow$ Green
	$P_s = $ `3` $\longrightarrow$ Yellow
	$P_s = $ `4` $\longrightarrow$ Blue
	$P_s = $ `5` $\longrightarrow$ Magenta
	$P_s = $ `6` $\longrightarrow$ Cyan
	$P_s = $ `7` $\longrightarrow$ White
`ESC [ 1 0 0 m`	Set default background and foreground colors
`ESC [ `P_s` n`	Device Status Report (DSR)
	$P_s = $ 5 $\longrightarrow$ Status Report `ESC [ 0 n` $\longrightarrow$ OK
	$P_s = $ 6 $\longrightarrow$ Report Cursor Position (CPR) [row;column] as `ESC [ `r` ; `c` R`
`ESC [ `P_s` ; `P_s` r`	Set Scrolling Region [top;bottom] (default = full size of window) (DECSTBM)
`ESC [ `P_s` x`	Request Terminal Parameters (DECREQTPARM)

ESC [? P_s h   DEC Private Mode Set (DECSET)

P_s = 1 → Application Cursor Keys (DECCKM)

P_s = 4 → Smooth (Slow) Scroll (DECSCLM)

P_s = 5 → Reverse Video (DECSCNM)

P_s = 6 → Origin Mode (DECOM)

P_s = 7 → Wraparound Mode (DECAWM)

P_s = 9 → Send MIT Mouse Row & Column on Button Press

P_s = 3 8 → Enter Tektronix mode (DECTEK)

P_s = 4 4 → Turn On Margin Bell

P_s = 4 5 → Reverse-wraparound Mode

P_s = 4 6 → Start Logging

P_s = 4 7 → Use Alternate Screen Buffer

ESC [? P_s l   DEC Private Mode Reset (DECRST)

P_s = 1 → Normal Cursor Keys (DECCKM)

P_s = 4 → Jump (Fast) Scroll (DECSCLM)

P_s = 5 → Normal Video (DECSCNM)

P_s = 6 → Normal Cursor Mode (DECOM)

P_s = 7 → No Wraparound Mode (DECAWM)

P_s = 9 → Don't Send MIT Mouse Row & Column on Button Press

P_s = 4 4 → Turn Off Margin Bell

P_s = 4 5 → No Reverse-wraparound Mode

P_s = 4 6 → Stop Logging

P_s = 4 7 → Use Normal Screen Buffer

ESC `[` `?` P_s `r` Restore DEC Private Mode

P_s = `1` ⟶ Normal/Application Cursor Keys (DECCKM)

P_s = `4` ⟶ Jump (Fast)/Smooth (Slow) Scroll (DECSCLM)

P_s = `5` ⟶ Normal/Reverse Video (DECSCNM)

P_s = `6` ⟶ Normal/Origin Cursor Mode (DECOM)

P_s = `7` ⟶ No Wraparound/Wraparound Mode (DECAWM)

P_s = `9` ⟶ Don't Send/Send MIT Mouse Row & Column on Button Press

P_s = `4` `4` ⟶ Turn Off/On Margin Bell

P_s = `4` `5` ⟶ No Reverse-wraparound/Reverse-wraparound Mode

P_s = `4` `6` ⟶ Stop/Start Logging

P_s = `4` `7` ⟶ Use Normal/Alternate Screen Buffer

ESC `[` `?` P_s `s` Save DEC Private Mode

P_s = `1` ⟶ Normal/Application Cursor Keys (DECCKM)

P_s = `4` ⟶ Jump (Fast)/Smooth (Slow) Scroll (DECSCLM)

P_s = `5` ⟶ Normal/Reverse Video (DECSCNM)

P_s = `6` ⟶ Normal/Origin Cursor Mode (DECOM)

P_s = `7` ⟶ No Wraparound/Wraparound Mode (DECAWM)

P_s = `9` ⟶ Don't Send/Send MIT Mouse Row & Column on Button Press

P_s = `4` `4` Turn Off/On Margin Bell

P_s = `4` `5` ⟶ No Reverse-wraparound/Reverse-wraparound Mode

P_s = `4` `6` ⟶ Stop/Start Logging

P_s = `4` `7` ⟶ Use Normal/Alternate Screen Buffer

ESC `]` P_s `;` P_t `BEL` Set Text Parameters

P_s = `0` ⟶ Change Window Name and Title to P_t

P_s = `1` ⟶ Change Window Name to P_t

P_s = `2` ⟶ Change Window Title to P_t

P_s = `4` `6` ⟶ Change Log File to P_t

ESC `c` Full Reset (RIS)

Additional xterm Control Sequences for Release 4

Tek Mode

ESC 7   Returns to VT102 mode, hides Tek window

VT102 Mode

ESC] 3; BEL   Disable window resizing (ignored with the **-rs** option or when
                         cursesResize is TRUE).

ESC] 4; BEL   Enable window resizing.

C Appendix C: .olfmrc Binding File

File Manager Application: Binding File

The OPEN LOOK File Manager application can be customized by the user. Customization is performed through the `.olfmrc` file. A sample `.olfmrc` file is installed in `/usr/X/clients/olfm`.

The BNF for the language accepted in the `.olfmrc` file is:

```
s = stmt { stmt };
stmtm = menu   on ;
menu = "menu" menuname(def) title { label action } ";";
on = "on" pattern { ";" pattern } menuname(use) action iconfile printcmd ";";
menuname = word ;
title = string ;
label = string ;
printcmd = string ;
pattern = string ;
iconfile = word ;
string = "′" word "′" ;
word = c { c } ;
c = <all ascii characters> - <',', ';', ''', SPACE, TAB, NL, '{','}'> ;
```

The "action" command is presumed to be the edit command for the type of file. The print command is presumed to be the command string needed to print the file.

The File Manager searches the user's home directory, then the directory `/usr/X/clients/olfm` for the `.olfmrc` file (for example, it tries to read the file `${HOME}/.olfmrc` first, then, if necessary, `/usr/X/clients/olfm/.olfmrc` to initialize the pop-up menus and file typing for the File Manager session.

New icon files can be created using the bitmap utility. Note: these bitmaps should be 24 x 24 pixels.

The File Manager uses the environment variable OLFMICONPATH to search for icon bitmaps named in the `rc` file. It is parsed as other PATH variables (for example, PATH, CDPATH). The File Manager appends a standard path `":/usr/X/clients/olfm/bitmaps"` to the value of this variable. If the variable is not set, the File Manager appends this to `""`, resulting in `":/usr/X/clients/olfm/bitmaps"` (for example, it will first look in the user's current (when the File Manager was started) directory, then the directory `/usr/X/clients/olfm/bitmaps`.

Glossary

Abbreviated scrollbar	A scrollbar that is used when a split pane is too small to display a complete scrollbar without a cable. The abbreviated scrollbar has cable anchors and up and down arrows.
Abbreviated menu button	A small square menu button with the label to the left and the current setting to the right. Abbreviated menu buttons function just like menu buttons.
Accelerator	A shortcut method of accessing controls, menus, and submenus, by typing characters on the keyboard. Accelerators are global to an operation and do not require active input focus in order to operate.
Active input area	The area of the screen that can accept text input from the keyboard.
Active input focus	The state of the window or text field that accepts text input from the keyboard.
ADJUST	The mouse button that is used to extend or reduce selections. The keyboard equivalent of this button is $\boxed{\text{Ctrl}}$ $\boxed{\text{\&}}$.
Application	A program that performs a specific task, such as a word processor or spreadsheet.
Automatic scrolling	When all of a file is not visible in a window, the operation in which the view in the pane automatically shifts to follow the pointer movement as you press SELECT and wipe it through the data.

Back	An item on the Window menu that is used to move selected windows or icons to the back of the screen.
Base window	The primary window for any application.
Basic pointer	An arrow pointing northwest that shows the mouse position.
Binding file	The *.olfmrc* file used by the File Manager application to define types and associate attributes with those types.
Border	The solid outline that surrounds a window or icon.
Bottom cable anchor	The button at the bottom of a scrollbar cable.
Busy pattern	A stippled pattern displayed in the header of a window or in the background of a button to show that the application is temporarily performing a function and cannot accept input.
Button	A one-selection element of a control area.
Cable	The part of the scrollbar that represents the total size of the data that you can view in the pane.
Cable anchor	The rectangular area at the end of the scrollbar cable.
Cancel	An item on a pop-up window menu, used to remove the pop-up window from the screen when it has settings that are changed but have not been applied.

Caret	The graphical representation of the insert point. The caret shows the insert point on a window that accepts keyboard input or on a text field. An active caret is a solid triangle that blinks. An inactive caret is a dimmed diamond.
Check box	A nonexclusive setting that shows a check mark in a square box when the setting is chosen.
Click	The act of pressing a mouse button once and releasing it without moving the pointer.
Client	An application.
Close	A selection on the Window menu that is used to change the visual representation of an application from a window to an icon.
Command button	A button that executes a single command.
Command item	An item on a menu that when selected executes a single command.
Command window	A pop-up window that is used to execute application commands or set parameters.
Control area	An unbordered region of a window where controls such as buttons and settings are displayed.
Controls	Objects in a control area and on a menu that are used to perform an action. Controls include items on windows, buttons, menu buttons, window buttons, exclusive and nonexclusive settings, sliders, and check boxes.

Default	The operation or function already supplied by the OPEN LOOK Interface, whether indicated as such by the system, or by the system administrator or user through customization. If you do not make a choice when it is offered, the default operation will take effect. A default menu item is outlined.
Default icon region	The edge of the screen the icon moves to the first time it is displayed.
Dimmed control	An inactive control that cannot accept input from the mouse or keyboard.
Dismiss	A selection on a pop-up window menu that removes the menu from the screen.
displaypkg	The command that displays the names of the software packages and version numbers installed on your computer.
Double-click	The act of clicking twice quickly with a mouse button; an accelerator that performs a specific function without using a menu.
Drag	The mouse movement that involves pressing and simultaneously holding a mouse button to move the pointer across the screen.
Drag area	The area in the middle of the scrollbar elevator or slider.
Elevator	The part of the scrollbar with up and down arrows and a drag area. The elevator "rides" the scrollbar cable.
End user	The user who is operating the OPEN LOOK Interface.

Ethernet	XEROX's trade name for a 10-Megabit coaxial local area network media.
Exclusive setting	A control used for mutually exclusive settings. The chosen setting is displayed with a bold outline.
Factory Default	The OPEN LOOK-supplied default setting.
File Manager	The OPEN LOOK Interface application that manages the UNIX file system.
Footer	The bottom area of a window. The footer is used by an application for information and error messages. This feature is application-supplied, so does not appear in every window.
Full Size	The maximum size of a window; also the item on a Window Menu that changes the size of a window to its maximum size.
Function keys	Numbered keys (F1, F2, etc.) located on the side or across the top of your keyboard, used to perform specific commands with a single keystroke.
Glyph	A picture or graphic representation of an object.
Header	The band across the top of every window. Each header has a centered title and window menu button.
Help	An OPEN LOOK Interface implementation that provides on-screen help. The application supplies help for application functions and elements.

Highlighting	A visual indication that an object is in a special state. In monochrome implementations, the visual indication is reverse video.
Hot spot	The place on the pointer glyph that determines the exact spot on the screen where an action is registered. The hot spot on the basic pointer is the tip of the arrow. In other cases, the hot spot may be in the middle of the glyph.
Icon	A small pictorial representation of a base window.
Icon region	The area on the Workspace where your icons appear. The default is the bottom of the screen.
Inactive control	A control that cannot accept input from the mouse or keyboard, and that is dimmed to show this state.
Insert point	The specific location in the active input area where keyboard input is displayed. A caret is displayed to mark the insert point.
installpkg	The command used to install software.
Menu button	A multiple-selection element of a control area. A submenu always accompanies a menu button.
Menu item	A multiple-selection element of a menu. A submenu always accompanies a menu item.
MENU	The mouse button used to display menus. The keyboard equivalent of this button is (Alt) (M) or (f4).

Mnemonics	One or more keystrokes that allow you to perform a screen function, such as accessing a menu. Mnemonics only work if the window you are in has active input focus and can accept keyboard input. Mnemonics allow you to perform functions using the keyboard rather than the mouse.
Modifier key	The keyboard key designated via the Keyboard Settings Workspace property window to work with a mouse button to perform a function. Modifier keys are: <SHIFT>, <CTRL>, <ALT>, <CAPS LOCK>, and <NUM LOCK>.
More arrow	A small nonscrollable triangle displayed at the end of text in the header or footer of a window that has been truncated during a resize operation.
More button	A square button with an arrowhead inside its border that allows you to scroll in a text or numeric field, present only when the text in the field cannot be completely displayed.
Mouse	An electronic or mechanical hand-held device used to select and manipulate information on a computer screen.
Mouse button	Any one of the three mouse buttons: SELECT, ADJUST, or MENU. Each button performs a specific function for manipulating windows or menus.
Multi-click	The act of clicking a mouse button rapidly a specified number of times. Multi-clicking is usually an accelerator for other functions.

Nonexclusive setting	A set of nonexclusive choices, indicated by separated rectangles. The chosen settings are surrounded by a bold outline.
Notice	A warning or error message display that must be addressed before you can proceed.
olinit	The command used to access the OPEN LOOK Interface.
Object	Any item, including menus, windows, icons, files, directories, glyphs, portions of text, or buttons, which can be manipulated by use of the pointer and mouse buttons.
Open	A selection on the Window Menu that is used to convert an icon to a window.
Pane	The rectangular area in a window where the application displays its data.
Pointer	Any graphic representation of the location of the mouse on the screen.
Pointer jumping	The automatic movement of the pointer to a specific location.
Pop-up menu	A menu that is displayed when you press MENU on any part of a window or the Workspace, but not on another menu.
Pop-up window menu	The menu that is displayed when you press MENU on the header of a pop-up window.
Pop-up window	A window that pops up to perform a specific function and then is dismissed. This includes command windows, property windows, and help windows.

Press	The act of pushing a mouse button without releasing it.
Program	See *application*.
Properties	Settable characteristics, such as the color of a window or the placement of icons.
Property window	A kind of pop-up window used to set properties associated with an object, an application, or a window.
Proportion indicator	The dark area of the scrollbar cable shows the proportion of data that is currently viewed in the pane, relative to the total length of the cable which represents the total size.
Pushpin	A graphic representation of a pushpin, which, when activated, keeps a menu, property window, or command window displayed on the screen.
Quit	To exit an application. Quit is also a selection on the Window menu, that quits the window.
Refresh	An item on the Window menu that redisplays the contents of selected windows or icons.
Resize corner	The corner of a window that can be dragged with a mouse button to enlarge or reduce the window.
Restore Size	The selection on a Window menu that changes a window from its maximum size to its previous size.
root	The superuser login ID. You must log in as root to install software or to perform system administration tasks.

Scrollbar	The control used to move the view of the data displayed in the pane.
Scrollbar Menu	The pop-up menu that is used to reposition the data in the pane.
Scrolling	The act of moving through data that cannot be viewed all at once in a pane.
Scrolling list	A pane containing a list of text fields that may be editable.
Select	To choose an object (or objects) on the screen that will be the subject of operation.
SELECT	The mouse button used to select objects, set the Insert point, manipulate controls, and drag objects. The keyboard equivalent of this button is <spacebar>.
Server	The part of the OPEN LOOK Interface that manages the video display and its windows, keyboard, and mouse.
Shrink	To resize a window so that its area is reduced.
Slider	The control used to set a numeric value and give a visual indication of the setting.
Stay-up menu	A menu that stays up on the screen when you click MENU, and remains on the screen until you make a choice or dismiss the menu.
StarLAN	AT&T trade name for a star network configuration that connects Local Area Networks.
Submenu	An additional menu that is displayed from a menu button or menu item.

Superuser	A user with administrative privileges and the root login.
Terminal Emulator	The application that emulates the DEC VT102 terminal on the AT&T 6386 WGS color console.
Text field	An area in a window in which you type text from the keyboard.
Title	The name of the application or function that is displayed at the top of a window or pop-up menu.
Top cable anchor	The button at the top of a scrollbar.
Unsupported applications	Applications that AT&T offers for demonstration and experimentation purposes only.
Validation	The application's verification that the contents of a text field are appropriate to the function.
Window button	A button that produces a window.
Window item	An item on a menu that when selected produces a window.
Window Manager	The application of the OPEN LOOK Interface that changes the sizes of windows, converts windows into icons, and performs other window operations.
Window Menu	The menu that is accessed from the window header.
Window menu button	The glyph that appears in the upper left corner of the header and on a button that displays a pop-up window.

Workspace

The background screen area on which windows and icons are displayed.

Workspace Manager

The application of the OPEN LOOK Interface that manages properties, displays windows, menus, and icons, and helps the system to manage other applications and execute programs.

Workspace Menu

The menu that controls global functions.

Workspace Property Window

The property window you access from the Workspace Menu, with which you customize your Workspace environment.

Index

OPEN LOOK GUI User's Guide: Release 4

RE